MznLnx

Missing Links Exam Preps

Exam Prep for

Brief Calculus and Its Applications

Goldstein & Lay & Schneider, 10th Edition

The MznLnx Exam Prep is your link from the texbook and lecture to your exams.
The MznLnx Exam Preps are unauthorized and comprehensive reviews of your textbooks.

All material provided by MznLnx and Rico Publications (c) 2010
Textbook publishers and textbook authors do not particpate in or contribute to these reviews.

MznLnx

Rico Publications

Exam Prep for Brief Calculus and Its Applications
10th Edition
Goldstein & Lay & Schneider

Publisher: Raymond Houge
Assistant Editor: Michael Rouger
Text and Cover Designer: Lisa Buckner
Marketing Manager: Sara Swagger
Project Manager, Editorial Production: Jerry Emerson
Art Director: Vernon Lowerui

Product Manager: Dave Mason
Editorial Assitant: Rachel Guzmanji
Pedagogy: Debra Long
Cover Image: Jim Reed/Getty Images
Text and Cover Printer: City Printing, Inc.
Compositor: Media Mix, Inc.

(c) 2010 Rico Publications

ALL RIGHTS RESERVED. No part of this work covered by the copyright may be reproduced or used in any form or by an means--graphic, electronic, or mechanical, including photocopying, recording, taping, Web distribution, information storage, and retrieval systems, or in any other manner--without the written permission of the publisher.

For more information about our products, contact us at:
Dave.Mason@RicoPublications.com

For permission to use material from this text or product, submit a request online to:
Dave.Mason@RicoPublications.com

Printed in the United States
ISBN:

Contents

CHAPTER 1
Functions — 1

CHAPTER 2
The Derivative — 18

CHAPTER 3
Applications of the Derivative — 29

CHAPTER 4
Techniques of Differentiation — 43

CHAPTER 5
Logarithm Functions — 53

CHAPTER 6
Applications of the Exponential and Natural Logarithm Functions — 62

CHAPTER 7
The Definite Integral — 73

CHAPTER 8
Functions of Several Variables — 89

CHAPTER 9
The Trigonometric Functions — 102

ANSWER KEY — 113

TO THE STUDENT

COMPREHENSIVE

The *MznLnx* Exam Prep series is designed to help you pass your exams. Editors at MznLnx review your textbooks and then prepare these practice exams to help you master the textbook material. Unlike study guides, workbooks, and practice tests provided by the texbook publisher and textbook authors, *MznLnx* gives you **all** of the material in each chapter in exam form, not just samples, so you can be sure to nail your exam.

MECHANICAL

The MznLnx Exam Prep series creates exams that will help you learn the subject matter as well as test you on your understanding. Each question is designed to help you master the concept. Just working through the exams, you gain an understanding of the subject--its a simple mechanical process that produces success.

INTEGRATED STUDY GUIDE AND REVIEW

MznLnx is not just a set of exams designed to test you, its also a comprehensive review of the subject content. Each exam question is also a review of the concept, making sure that you will get the answer correct without having to go to other sources of material. You learn as you go! Its the easiest way to pass an exam.

HUMOR

Studying can be tedious and dry. MznLnx's instructional design includes moderate humor within the exam questions on occassion, to break the tedium and revitalize the brain

Chapter 1. Functions

1. The mathematical concept of a _____ expresses the intuitive idea of deterministic dependence between two quantities, one of which is viewed as primary and the other as secondary. A _____ then is a way to associate a unique output for each input of a specified type, for example, a real number or an element of a given set.
   - a. Function0
   - b. Thing
   - c. Undefined
   - d. Undefined

2. _____ are the basic objects of study in graph theory. Informally speaking, a graph is a set of objects called points, nodes, or vertices connected by links called lines or edges.
   - a. Graphs0
   - b. Thing
   - c. Undefined
   - d. Undefined

3. In mathematics, a _____ may be described informally as a number that can be given by an infinite decimal representation.
   - a. Thing
   - b. Real number0
   - c. Undefined
   - d. Undefined

4. A _____ is a one-dimensional picture in which the integers are shown as specially-marked points evenly spaced on a line.
   - a. Number line0
   - b. Thing
   - c. Undefined
   - d. Undefined

5. In mathematics, a _____ number is a number which can be expressed as a ratio of two integers. Non-integer _____ numbers (commonly called fractions) are usually written as the vulgar fraction a / b, where b is not zero.
   - a. Thing
   - b. Rational0
   - c. Undefined
   - d. Undefined

6. _____ is the state of being greater than any finite real or natural number, however large.
   - a. Infinite0
   - b. Thing
   - c. Undefined
   - d. Undefined

7. A _____ decimal is a number whose decimal representation eventually becomes periodic (i.e. the same number sequence _____ indefinitely).
   - a. Repeating0
   - b. Thing
   - c. Undefined
   - d. Undefined

8. In mathematics, a set is called _____ if there is a bijection between the set and some set of the form {1, 2, ..., n} where n is a natural number.
   - a. Thing
   - b. Finite0
   - c. Undefined
   - d. Undefined

9. In mathematics, an _____ number is any real number that is not a rational number- that is, it is a number which cannot be expressed as a fraction m/n, where m and n are integers.
   - a. Irrational0
   - b. Thing
   - c. Undefined
   - d. Undefined

10. In mathematics, an _____ is any real number that is not a rational number ¡ª that is, it is a number which cannot be expressed as m/n, where m and n are integers.

a. Thing
b. Irrational number0
c. Undefined
d. Undefined

11. In mathematics, an _____ is a statement about the relative size or order of two objects.
   a. Thing
   b. Inequality0
   c. Undefined
   d. Undefined

12. In mathematics, _____ are any real number that is not a rational number ¡ª that is, it is a number which cannot be expressed as m/n, where m and n are integers.
   a. Thing
   b. Irrational numbers0
   c. Undefined
   d. Undefined

13. The _____, the average in everyday English, which is also called the arithmetic _____ (and is distinguished from the geometric _____ or harmonic _____). The average is also called the sample _____. The expected value of a random variable, which is also called the population _____.
   a. Mean0
   b. Thing
   c. Undefined
   d. Undefined

14. In geometry, a line _____ is a part of a line that is bounded by two end points, and contains every point on the line between its end points.
   a. Concept
   b. Segment0
   c. Undefined
   d. Undefined

15. In geometry, an _____ is a point at which a line segment or ray terminates.
   a. Thing
   b. Endpoint0
   c. Undefined
   d. Undefined

16. A _____ is a part of a line that is bounded by two end points, and contains every point on the line between its end points.
   a. Line segment0
   b. Thing
   c. Undefined
   d. Undefined

17. In elementary algebra, an _____ is a set that contains every real number between two indicated numbers and may contain the two numbers themselves.
   a. Interval0
   b. Thing
   c. Undefined
   d. Undefined

18. In Euclidean geometry, a _____ is the set of all points in a plane at a fixed distance, called the radius, from a given point, the center.
   a. Circle0
   b. Thing
   c. Undefined
   d. Undefined

19. In mathematics, _____ geometry was the traditional name for the geometry of three-dimensional Euclidean space — for practical purposes the kind of space we live in.

a. Thing
b. Solid0
c. Undefined
d. Undefined

20. _____, from Latin meaning "to make progress", is defined in two different ways. Pure economic _____ is the increase in wealth that an investor has from making an investment, taking into consideration all costs associated with that investment including the opportunity cost of capital.
    a. Profit0
    b. Thing
    c. Undefined
    d. Undefined

21. A _____ is a symbolic representation denoting a quantity or expression. It often represents an "unknown" quantity that has the potential to change.
    a. Thing
    b. Variable0
    c. Undefined
    d. Undefined

22. In mathematics, an inequality is a statement about the relative size or order of two objects. For example 14 > 10, or 14 is _____ 10.
    a. Greater than0
    b. Thing
    c. Undefined
    d. Undefined

23. The _____ of measurement are a globally standardized and modernized form of the metric system.
    a. Thing
    b. Units0
    c. Undefined
    d. Undefined

24. Equivalence is the condition of being _____ or essentially equal.
    a. Thing
    b. Equivalent0
    c. Undefined
    d. Undefined

25. In mathematics, an _____ is any of the arguments, i.e. "inputs", to a function. Thus if we have a function f(x), then x is a _____.
    a. Thing
    b. Independent variable0
    c. Undefined
    d. Undefined

26. In mathematics, a _____ of a k-place relation $L \subseteq X_1 \times ... \times X_k$ is one of the sets X_j, $1 \leq j \leq k$. In the special case where k = 2 and $L \subseteq X_1 \times X_2$ is a function $L : X_1 \to X_2$, it is conventional to refer to X_1 as the _____ of the function and to refer to X_2 as the codomain of the function.
    a. Thing
    b. Domain0
    c. Undefined
    d. Undefined

27. In mathematics, the _____ of a function is the set of all "output" values produced by that function. Given a function $f : A \to B$, the _____ of f, is defined to be the set $\{x \in B : x = f(a) \text{ for some } a \in A\}$.
    a. Range0
    b. Thing
    c. Undefined
    d. Undefined

28. _____ is a special mathematical relationship between two quantities. Two quantities are called proportional if they vary in such a way that one of the quantities is a constant multiple of the other, or equivalently if they have a constant ratio.

a. Thing
b. Proportionality0
c. Undefined
d. Undefined

29. A _____ is a three-dimensional solid object bounded by six square faces, facets, or sides, with three meeting at each vertex.
   a. Thing
   b. Cube0
   c. Undefined
   d. Undefined

30. A _____ is a deliberate process for transforming one or more inputs into one or more results.
   a. Thing
   b. Calculation0
   c. Undefined
   d. Undefined

31. The payment of _____ as remuneration for services rendered or products sold is a common way to reward sales people.
   a. Thing
   b. Commission0
   c. Undefined
   d. Undefined

32. _____ is a kind of property which exists as magnitude or multitude. It is among the basic classes of things along with quality, substance, change, and relation.
   a. Thing
   b. Amount0
   c. Undefined
   d. Undefined

33. An _____ is a combination of numbers, operators, grouping symbols and/or free variables and bound variables arranged in a meaningful way which can be evaluated..
   a. Expression0
   b. Thing
   c. Undefined
   d. Undefined

34. In mathematics, the concept of a _____ tries to capture the intuitive idea of a geometrical one-dimensional and continuous object. A simple example is the circle.
   a. Curve0
   b. Thing
   c. Undefined
   d. Undefined

35. In geographic information systems, a _____ comprises an entity with a geographic location, typically determined by points, arcs, or polygons. Carriageways and cadastres exemplify _____ data.
   a. Thing
   b. Feature0
   c. Undefined
   d. Undefined

36. In Euclidean geometry, a uniform _____ is a linear transformation that enlargers or diminishes objects, and whose _____ factor is the same in all directions. This is also called homothethy.
   a. Scale0
   b. Thing
   c. Undefined
   d. Undefined

37. _____ is a mathematical subject that includes the study of limits, derivatives, integrals, and power series and constitutes a major part of modern university curriculum.

a. Calculus0
b. Thing
c. Undefined
d. Undefined

38. In a function the _____, is the variable which is the value, i.e. the "output", of the function.
a. Thing
b. Dependent variable0
c. Undefined
d. Undefined

39. In mathematics, the _____ f is the collection of all ordered pairs . In particular, graph means the graphical representation of this collection, in the form of a curve or surface, together with axes, etc. Graphing on a Cartesian plane is sometimes referred to as curve sketching.
a. Graph of a function0
b. Thing
c. Undefined
d. Undefined

40. In mathematics, _____ are the intuitive idea of a geometrical one-dimensional and continuous object.
a. Thing
b. Curves0
c. Undefined
d. Undefined

41. _____ is a test to determine if a relation or its graph is a function or not
a. Vertical line test0
b. Thing
c. Undefined
d. Undefined

42. Acid _____ ratio measures the ability of a company to use its near cash or quick assets to immediately extinguish its current liabilities.
a. Thing
b. Test0
c. Undefined
d. Undefined

43. Mathematical _____ is used to represent ideas.
a. Thing
b. Notation0
c. Undefined
d. Undefined

44. A _____ signifies a point or points of probability on a subject e.g., the _____ of creativity, which allows for the formation of rule or norm or law by interpretation of the phenomena events that can be created.
a. Thing
b. Principle0
c. Undefined
d. Undefined

45. A _____ function is a function for which, intuitively, small changes in the input result in small changes in the output.
a. Continuous0
b. Event
c. Undefined
d. Undefined

46. In mathematics, a _____ is an ordered list of objects. Like a set, it contains members, also called elements or terms, and the number of terms is called the length of the _____. Unlike a set, order matters, and the exact same elements can appear multiple times at different positions in the _____.
a. Thing
b. Sequence0
c. Undefined
d. Undefined

47. _____ is a synonym for information.
   a. Data0
   b. Thing
   c. Undefined
   d. Undefined

48. The word _____ comes from the Latin word linearis, which means created by lines.
   a. Thing
   b. Linear0
   c. Undefined
   d. Undefined

49. A _____ defined function f(x) of a real variable x is a function whose definition is given differently on disjoint subsets of its domain.
   a. Piecewise0
   b. Thing
   c. Undefined
   d. Undefined

50. In physics, _____ is an influence that may cause an object to accelerate. It may be experienced as a lift, a push, or a pull. The actual acceleration of the body is determined by the vector sum of all forces acting on it, known as net _____ or resultant _____.
   a. Thing
   b. Force0
   c. Undefined
   d. Undefined

51. In the scientific method, an _____ (Latin: ex-+-periri, "of (or from) trying"), is a set of actions and observations, performed in the context of solving a particular problem or question, in order to support or falsify a hypothesis or research concerning phenomena.
   a. Thing
   b. Experiment0
   c. Undefined
   d. Undefined

52. In mathematics and the mathematical sciences, a _____ is a fixed, but possibly unspecified, value. This is in contrast to a variable, which is not fixed.
   a. Constant0
   b. Thing
   c. Undefined
   d. Undefined

53. A _____ is a set of numbers that designate location in a given reference system, such as x,y in a planar _____ system or an x,y,z in a three-dimensional _____ system.
   a. Coordinate0
   b. Thing
   c. Undefined
   d. Undefined

54. A _____ is a number that is less than zero.
   a. Negative number0
   b. Thing
   c. Undefined
   d. Undefined

55. A _____ is an equation in which each term is either a constant or the product of a constant times the first power of a variable.
   a. Linear equation0
   b. Thing
   c. Undefined
   d. Undefined

56. A _____ is a first degree polynomial mathematical function of the form: f(x) = mx + b where m and b are real constants and x is a real variable.

Chapter 1. Functions

a. Linear function0
b. Thing
c. Undefined
d. Undefined

57. In astronomy, geography, geometry and related sciences and contexts, a plane is said to be _____ at a given point if it is locally perpendicular to the gradient of the gravity field, i.e., with the direction of the gravitational force at that point.
a. Thing
b. Horizontal0
c. Undefined
d. Undefined

58. _____ is a function whose values do not vary and thus are constant.
a. Constant function0
b. Thing
c. Undefined
d. Undefined

59. In mathematics, a _____ is the result of multiplying, or an expression that identifies factors to be multiplied.
a. Product0
b. Thing
c. Undefined
d. Undefined

60. A _____ is a type of debt. All material things can be lent but this article focuses exclusively on monetary loans. Like all debt instruments, a _____ entails the redistribution of financial assets over time, between the lender and the borrower.
a. Thing
b. Loan0
c. Undefined
d. Undefined

61. _____, in law and economics, is a form of risk management primarily used to hedge against the risk of a contingent loss.
a. Thing
b. Insurance0
c. Undefined
d. Undefined

62. Fixed costs are expenses whose total does not change in proportion to the activity of a business.Unit fixed costs decline with volume following a retangular hyperbola as the volume of production.Variable costs by contrast change in relation to the activity of a business such as sales or production volume.Along with variable costs,fixed costs make up one of the two components of total cost. In the most simple production function total cost is equal to fixed costs plus variable costs.In accounting terminology, fixed costs will broadly include all costs which are not included in cost of goods sold, and variable costs are those captured in costs of goods sold. The implicit assumption required to make the equivalence between the accounting and economics terminology is that the accounting period is equal to the period in which fixed costs do not vary in relation to production. In practice, this equivalence does not always hold and depending on the period under consideration by management, some overhead expenses can be adjusted by management, and the specific allocation of each expense to each category will be decided under cost accounting.In business planning and management accounting, usage of the terms fixed costs, variable costs and others will often differ from usage in economics, and may depend on the intended use. For example, costs may be segregated into per unit costs fixed costs per period, and variable costs as a proportion of revenue. Capital expenditures will usually be allocated separately, and depending on the purpose, a portion may be regularly allocated to expenses as depreciation and amortization and seen as a _____ per period, or the entire amount may be considered upfront fixed costs.
a. Thing
b. Fixed cost0
c. Undefined
d. Undefined

63. _____ are expenses whose total does not change in proportion to the activity of a business, within the relevant time period or scale of production
   a. Fixed costs0
   b. Thing
   c. Undefined
   d. Undefined

64. Any point where a graph makes contact with an coordinate axis is called an _____ of the graph
   a. Thing
   b. Intercept0
   c. Undefined
   d. Undefined

65. A _____ is a polynomial function of the form $f(x) = ax^2 + bx + c$, where a, b, c are real numbers and a , 0.
   a. Quadratic function0
   b. Event
   c. Undefined
   d. Undefined

66. In mathematics, an _____, mean, or central tendency of a data set refers to a measure of the "middle" or "expected" value of the data set.
   a. Average0
   b. Concept
   c. Undefined
   d. Undefined

67. _____ is the application of tools and a processing medium to the transformation of raw materials into finished goods for sale.
   a. Thing
   b. Manufacturing0
   c. Undefined
   d. Undefined

68. In topology and related areas of mathematics a _____ or Moore-Smith sequence is a generalization of a sequence, intended to unify the various notions of limit and generalize them to arbitrary topological spaces.
   a. Thing
   b. Net0
   c. Undefined
   d. Undefined

69. In mathematics, the _____ is a conic section generated by the intersection of a right circular conical surface and a plane parallel to a generating straight line of that surface. It can also be defined as locus of points in a plane which are equidistant from a given point.
   a. Parabola0
   b. Thing
   c. Undefined
   d. Undefined

70. In mathematics, a _____ is an expression that is constructed from one or more variables and constants, using only the operations of addition, subtraction, multiplication, and constant positive whole number exponents. is a _____. Note in particular that division by an expression containing a variable is not in general allowed in polynomials. [1]
   a. Thing
   b. Polynomial0
   c. Undefined
   d. Undefined

71. The _____ integers are all the integers from zero on upwards.
   a. Nonnegative0
   b. Thing
   c. Undefined
   d. Undefined

72. In mathematics, a _____ is the end result of a division problem. It can also be expressed as the number of times the divisor divides into the dividend.

a. Quotient0
c. Undefined
b. Thing
d. Undefined

73. In mathematics, a _____ is any function which can be written as the ratio of two polynomial functions.
    a. Thing
    b. Rational function0
    c. Undefined
    d. Undefined

74. _____ has many meanings, most of which simply .
    a. Thing
    b. Power0
    c. Undefined
    d. Undefined

75. In mathematics, the _____ (or modulus) of a real number is its numerical value without regard to its sign.
    a. Thing
    b. Absolute value0
    c. Undefined
    d. Undefined

76. In statistics, _____ means the most frequent value assumed by a random variable, or occurring in a sampling of a random variable.
    a. Concept
    b. Mode0
    c. Undefined
    d. Undefined

77. In mathematics, defined and _____ are used to explain whether or not expressions have meaningful, sensible, and unambiguous values.
    a. Undefined0
    b. Thing
    c. Undefined
    d. Undefined

78. _____ variables are variables other than the independent variable that may bear any effect on the behavior of the subject being studied.
    a. Thing
    b. Extraneous0
    c. Undefined
    d. Undefined

79. _____ is a term used in accounting, economics and finance with reference to the fact that assets with finite lives lose value over time.
    a. Thing
    b. Depreciation0
    c. Undefined
    d. Undefined

80. A _____ is a unit of length, usually used to measure distance, in a number of different systems, including Imperial units, United States customary units and Norwegian/Swedish mil. Its size can vary from system to system, but in each is between 1 and 10 kilometers. In contemporary English contexts _____ refers to either:
    a. Thing
    b. Mile0
    c. Undefined
    d. Undefined

81. _____ is the transport of people on a trip/journey or the process or time involved in a person or object moving from one location to another.
    a. Thing
    b. Travel0
    c. Undefined
    d. Undefined

82. _____ is a unit of speed, expressing the number of international miles covered per hour.
   a. Miles per hour0   b. Thing
   c. Undefined   d. Undefined

83. _____, Greek for "knowledge of nature," is the branch of science concerned with the discovery and characterization of universal laws which govern matter, energy, space, and time.
   a. Thing   b. Physics0
   c. Undefined   d. Undefined

84. _____ is a branch of mathematics concerning the study of structure, relation and quantity.
   a. Concept   b. Algebra0
   c. Undefined   d. Undefined

85. _____ is a business term for the amount of money that a company receives from its activities in a given period, mostly from sales of products and/or services to customers
   a. Thing   b. Revenue0
   c. Undefined   d. Undefined

86. The plus and _____ signs are mathematical symbols used to represent the notions of positive and negative as well as the operations of addition and subtraction.
   a. Thing   b. Minus0
   c. Undefined   d. Undefined

87. In mathematics, _____ is an elementary arithmetic operation. When one of the numbers is a whole number, _____ is the repeated sum of the other number.
   a. Thing   b. Multiplication0
   c. Undefined   d. Undefined

88. A _____ is the part of a fraction that tells how many equal parts make up a whole, and which is used in the name of the fraction: "halves", "thirds", "fourths" or "quarters", "fifths" and so on.
   a. Concept   b. Denominator0
   c. Undefined   d. Undefined

89. A _____ is a numeral used to indicate a count. The most common use of the word today is to name the part of a fraction that tells the number or count of equal parts.
   a. Numerator0   b. Thing
   c. Undefined   d. Undefined

90. In sociology and biology a _____ is the collection of people or organisms of a particular species living in a given geographic area or space, usually measured by a census.
   a. Thing   b. Population0
   c. Undefined   d. Undefined

91. A _____ number is a positive integer which has a positive divisor other than one or itself.

Chapter 1. Functions

a. Composite0
b. Thing
c. Undefined
d. Undefined

92. A _____ is 360° or 2𝛿 radians.
   a. Thing
   b. Turn0
   c. Undefined
   d. Undefined

93. In linear algebra, the _____ of an n-by-n square matrix A is defined to be the sum of the elements on the main diagonal of A,
   a. Thing
   b. Trace0
   c. Undefined
   d. Undefined

94. A quadratic equation with real solutions, called roots, which may be real or complex, is given by the _____: $x = \frac{-b \pm \sqrt{b^2 - 4ac}}{2a}$.
   a. Thing
   b. Quadratic formula0
   c. Undefined
   d. Undefined

95. In mathematics, _____ is the decomposition of an object into a product of other objects, or factors, which when multiplied together give the original.
   a. Thing
   b. Factoring0
   c. Undefined
   d. Undefined

96. In mathematics, a _____ is a polynomial equation of the second degree. The general form is $ax^2 + bx + c = 0$.
   a. Thing
   b. Quadratic equation0
   c. Undefined
   d. Undefined

97. In mathematics, a _____ of a complex-valued function f is a member x of the domain of f such that f(x) vanishes at x, that is, $x : f(x) = 0$.
   a. Thing
   b. Root0
   c. Undefined
   d. Undefined

98. In plane geometry, a _____ is a polygon with four equal sides, four right angles, and parallel opposite sides. In algebra, the _____ of a number is that number multiplied by itself.
   a. Thing
   b. Square0
   c. Undefined
   d. Undefined

99. In mathematics, a _____ of a number x is a number r such that $r^2 = x$, or in words, a number r whose square (the result of multiplying the number by itself) is x.
   a. Square root0
   b. Thing
   c. Undefined
   d. Undefined

100. _____ traditionally refers to the statistical process of determining comparable scores on different forms of an exam
   a. Equating0
   b. Thing
   c. Undefined
   d. Undefined

101. In mathematics, the _____ of two sets A and B is the set that contains all elements of A that also belong to B (or equivalently, all elements of B that also belong to A), but no other elements.
   a. Intersection0
   b. Thing
   c. Undefined
   d. Undefined

102. In mathematics, factorization (British English: factorisation) or factoring is the decomposition of an object (for example, a number, a polynomial, or a matrix) into a product of other objects, or _____, which when multiplied together give the original.
   a. Factors0
   b. Thing
   c. Undefined
   d. Undefined

103. A _____ is the result of the addition of a set of numbers. The numbers may be natural numbers, complex numbers, matrices, or still more complicated objects. An infinite _____ is a subtle procedure known as a series.
   a. Thing
   b. Sum0
   c. Undefined
   d. Undefined

104. In mathematics, a _____ is a constant multiplicative factor of a certain object. The object can be such things as a variable, a vector, a function, etc. For example, the _____ of $9x^2$ is 9.
   a. Coefficient0
   b. Thing
   c. Undefined
   d. Undefined

105. _____ is a fixed, but possibly unspecified, value. This is in contrast to a variable, which is not fixed.
   a. Thing
   b. Constant term0
   c. Undefined
   d. Undefined

106. The _____ are the only integral domain whose positive elements are well-ordered, and in which order is preserved by addition. Like the natural numbers, the _____ form a countably infinite set. The set of all _____ is usually denoted in mathematics by a boldface Z .
   a. Integers0
   b. Thing
   c. Undefined
   d. Undefined

107. _____ is the largest positive integer that divides both numbers without remainder.
   a. Common Factor0
   b. Thing
   c. Undefined
   d. Undefined

108. A _____ is a negotiable instrument instructing a financial institution to pay a specific amount of a specific currency from a specific demand account held in the maker/depositor's name with that institution. Both the maker and payee may be natural persons or legal entities.
   a. Thing
   b. Check0
   c. Undefined
   d. Undefined

109. A _____ of a number is the product of that number with any integer.
   a. Thing
   b. Multiple0
   c. Undefined
   d. Undefined

Chapter 1. Functions

110. _____ or arithmetics is the oldest and most elementary branch of mathematics, used by almost everyone, for tasks ranging from simple daily counting to advanced science and business calculations.
   a. Arithmetic0
   b. Thing
   c. Undefined
   d. Undefined

111. _____ is a mathematical operation, written a^n, involving two numbers, the base a and the exponent n.
   a. Thing
   b. Exponentiating0
   c. Undefined
   d. Undefined

112. _____ is a mathematical operation, written a^n, involving two numbers, the base a and the exponent n.
   a. Exponentiation0
   b. Thing
   c. Undefined
   d. Undefined

113. _____ is the fee paid on borrowed money.
   a. Interest0
   b. Thing
   c. Undefined
   d. Undefined

114. _____ interest refers to the fact that whenever interest is calculated, it is based not only on the original principal, but also on any unpaid interest that has been added to the principal.
   a. Compound0
   b. Thing
   c. Undefined
   d. Undefined

115. _____ refers to the fact that whenever interest is calculated, it is based not only on the original principal, but also on any unpaid interest that has been added to the principal. The more frequently interest is compounded, the faster the balance grows.
   a. Concept
   b. Compound interest0
   c. Undefined
   d. Undefined

116. A _____ are accounts maintained by commercial banks, savings and loan associations, credit unions, and mutual savings banks that pay interest but can not be used directly as money by, for example, writing a cheque.
   a. Savings account0
   b. Thing
   c. Undefined
   d. Undefined

117. In business, particularly accounting, a _____ is the time intervals that the accounts, statement, payments, or other calculations cover.
   a. Thing
   b. Period0
   c. Undefined
   d. Undefined

118. A _____ is a special kind of ratio, indicating a relationship between two measurements with different units, such as miles to gallons or cents to pounds.
   a. Thing
   b. Rate0
   c. Undefined
   d. Undefined

119. _____ is a way of expressing a number as a fraction of 100 per cent meaning "per hundred".

Chapter 1. Functions

    a. Percent0
    c. Undefined
    b. Thing
    d. Undefined

120. An _____ is the fee paid on borrow money.
    a. Interest rate0
    c. Undefined
    b. Concept
    d. Undefined

121. _____ generally derives from name. A _____ quantity e.g., length, diameter, volume, voltage, value is generally the quantity according to which some item has been named or is generally referred to.
    a. Thing
    c. Undefined
    b. Nominal0
    d. Undefined

122. _____ finance, in finance, a debt security, issued by Issuer
    a. Thing
    c. Undefined
    b. Bond0
    d. Undefined

123. In mathematics, _____ growth occurs when the growth rate of a function is always proportional to the function's current size.
    a. Exponential0
    c. Undefined
    b. Thing
    d. Undefined

124. _____ or investing is a term with several closely-related meanings in business management, finance and economics, related to saving or deferring consumption.
    a. Investment0
    c. Undefined
    b. Thing
    d. Undefined

125. _____, either of the curved-bracket punctuation marks that together make a set of _____
    a. Thing
    c. Undefined
    b. Parentheses0
    d. Undefined

126. _____ is a notation for writing numbers that is often used by scientists and mathematicians to make it easier to write large and small numbers.
    a. Thing
    c. Undefined
    b. Scientific notation0
    d. Undefined

127. In mathematics, _____ expressions is used to reduce the expression into the lowest possible term.
    a. Thing
    c. Undefined
    b. Simplifying0
    d. Undefined

128. _____ is the symbol used to indicate the nth root of a number
    a. Radical0
    c. Undefined
    b. Thing
    d. Undefined

129. In mathematics, _____ are used to indicate the square root of a number.

Chapter 1. Functions

    a. Radicals0   b. Thing
    c. Undefined   d. Undefined

130. In geometry, a _____ is defined as a quadrilateral where all four of its angles are right angles.
    a. Rectangle0   b. Thing
    c. Undefined   d. Undefined

131. _____ is the distance around a given two-dimensional object. As a general rule, the _____ of a polygon can always be calculated by adding all the length of the sides together. So, the formula for triangles is P = a + b + c, where a, b and c stand for each side of it. For quadrilaterals the equation is P = a + b + c + d. For equilateral polygons, P = na, where n is the number of sides and a is the side length.
    a. Thing   b. Perimeter0
    c. Undefined   d. Undefined

132. In mathematics, a _____ is a two-dimensional manifold or surface that is perfectly flat.
    a. Thing   b. Plane0
    c. Undefined   d. Undefined

133. A _____ (or shape) refers to the external two-dimensional outline, appearance or configuration of some thing - in contrast to the matter or content or substance of which it is composed.
    a. Plane figure0   b. Thing
    c. Undefined   d. Undefined

134. The metre (or _____, see spelling differences) is a measure of length. It is the basic unit of length in the metric system and in the International System of Units (SI), used around the world for general and scientific purposes.
    a. Meter0   b. Concept
    c. Undefined   d. Undefined

135. In geometry, _____ angles are angles that have a common ray coming out of the vertex going between two other rays.
    a. Concept   b. Adjacent0
    c. Undefined   d. Undefined

136. The _____ of a solid object is the three-dimensional concept of how much space it occupies, often quantified numerically.
    a. Volume0   b. Thing
    c. Undefined   d. Undefined

137. In mathematics, a _____ is a quadric surface, with the following equation in Cartesian coordinates: $(x/a)^2 + (y/b)^2 = 1$.
    a. Thing   b. Cylinder0
    c. Undefined   d. Undefined

138. _____ are cubes in which all sides are of the same length and all face perpendicular to each other including an atom at each corner of the unigt cell.

16   Chapter 1. Functions

    a. Thing　　　　　　　　　　　　　　　　　　b. Cubic units0
    c. Undefined　　　　　　　　　　　　　　　　d. Undefined

139. In common philosophical language, a proposition or _____, is the content of an assertion, that is, it is true-or-false and defined by the meaning of a particular piece of language.
    a. Statement0　　　　　　　　　　　　　　　b. Concept
    c. Undefined　　　　　　　　　　　　　　　　d. Undefined

140. A _____ is an instrument used in geometry technical drawing and engineering/building to measure distances and/or to rule straight lines.
    a. Ruler0　　　　　　　　　　　　　　　　　　b. Thing
    c. Undefined　　　　　　　　　　　　　　　　d. Undefined

141. The _____ is the distance around a closed curve. _____ is a kind of perimeter.
    a. Circumference0　　　　　　　　　　　　　b. Thing
    c. Undefined　　　　　　　　　　　　　　　　d. Undefined

142. In classical geometry, a _____ of a circle or sphere is any line segment from its center to its boundary. By extension, the _____ of a circle or sphere is the length of any such segment. The _____ is half the diameter. In science and engineering the term _____ of curvature is commonly used as a synonym for _____.
    a. Radius0　　　　　　　　　　　　　　　　　b. Thing
    c. Undefined　　　　　　　　　　　　　　　　d. Undefined

143. There are two simple _____ the greatest common factor and least common multiple: standard factorization and prime factorization.
    a. Thing　　　　　　　　　　　　　　　　　　b. Methods for finding0
    c. Undefined　　　　　　　　　　　　　　　　d. Undefined

144. A _____ is the quantity that defines certain relatively constant characteristics of systems or functions..
    a. Thing　　　　　　　　　　　　　　　　　　b. Parameter0
    c. Undefined　　　　　　　　　　　　　　　　d. Undefined

145. _____ the expected value of a random variable displays the average or central value of the variable.It is a summary value of the distribution of the variable.
    a. Determining0　　　　　　　　　　　　　　b. Thing
    c. Undefined　　　　　　　　　　　　　　　　d. Undefined

146. In topology, the _____ are subsets S of a topological space X is the set of points which can be approached both from S and from the outside of S.
    a. Boundaries0　　　　　　　　　　　　　　　b. Thing
    c. Undefined　　　　　　　　　　　　　　　　d. Undefined

147. A _____, scatter diagram or scatter graph is a chart that uses Cartesian coordinates to display values for two variables.

a. Thing
b. Scatter plot0
c. Undefined
d. Undefined

148. _____ is a graph of the points representing a collection of data.
a. Thing
b. Scatter plots0
c. Undefined
d. Undefined

149. _____ are rectangular tables (or grids) of information, often financial information.
a. Thing
b. Spreadsheets0
c. Undefined
d. Undefined

150. A _____ is the part of the dividend that is left over when the dividend is not evenly divisible by the divisor.
a. Remainder0
b. Thing
c. Undefined
d. Undefined

Chapter 2. The Derivative

1. A _____ is a special kind of ratio, indicating a relationship between two measurements with different units, such as miles to gallons or cents to pounds.
   a. Thing
   b. Rate0
   c. Undefined
   d. Undefined

2. A _____ is a function that assigns a number to subsets of a given set.
   a. Thing
   b. Measure0
   c. Undefined
   d. Undefined

3. The _____ is a measurement of how a function changes when the values of its inputs change.
   a. Thing
   b. Derivative0
   c. Undefined
   d. Undefined

4. _____ is a set, with some particular properties and usually some additional structure, such as the operations of addition or multiplication, for instance.
   a. Thing
   b. Space0
   c. Undefined
   d. Undefined

5. In the scientific method, an _____ (Latin: ex-+-periri, "of (or from) trying"), is a set of actions and observations, performed in the context of solving a particular problem or question, in order to support or falsify a hypothesis or research concerning phenomena.
   a. Experiment0
   b. Thing
   c. Undefined
   d. Undefined

6. The mathematical concept of a _____ expresses the intuitive idea of deterministic dependence between two quantities, one of which is viewed as primary and the other as secondary. A _____ then is a way to associate a unique output for each input of a specified type, for example, a real number or an element of a given set.
   a. Function0
   b. Thing
   c. Undefined
   d. Undefined

7. _____ is often used to describe the measurement of the steepness, incline, gradient, or grade of a straight line. The _____ is defined as the ratio of the "rise" divided by the "run" between two points on a line, or in other words, the ratio of the altitude change to the horizontal distance between any two points on the line.
   a. Slope0
   b. Thing
   c. Undefined
   d. Undefined

8. The _____ of measurement are a globally standardized and modernized form of the metric system.
   a. Thing
   b. Units0
   c. Undefined
   d. Undefined

9. In business, _____, _____ cost or _____ expense refers to an ongoing expense of operating a business.
   a. Overhead0
   b. Thing
   c. Undefined
   d. Undefined

10. _____, in law and economics, is a form of risk management primarily used to hedge against the risk of a contingent loss.

a. Thing
b. Insurance0
c. Undefined
d. Undefined

11. Fixed costs are expenses whose total does not change in proportion to the activity of a business.Unit fixed costs decline with volume following a retangular hyperbola as the volume of production.Variable costs by contrast change in relation to the activity of a business such as sales or production volume.Along with variable costs,fixed costs make up one of the two components of total cost. In the most simple production function total cost is equal to fixed costs plus variable costs.In accounting terminology, fixed costs will broadly include all costs which are not included in cost of goods sold, and variable costs are those captured in costs of goods sold. The implicit assumption required to make the equivalence between the accounting and economics terminology is that the accounting period is equal to the period in which fixed costs do not vary in relation to production. In practice, this equivalence does not always hold and depending on the period under consideration by management, some overhead expenses can be adjusted by management, and the specific allocation of each expense to each category will be decided under cost accounting.In business planning and management accounting, usage of the terms fixed costs, variable costs and others will often differ from usage in economics, and may depend on the intended use. For example, costs may be segregated into per unit costs fixed costs per period, and variable costs as a proportion of revenue. Capital expenditures will usually be allocated separately, and depending on the purpose, a portion may be regularly allocated to expenses as depreciation and amortization and seen as a _____ per period, or the entire amount may be considered upfront fixed costs.
a. Thing
b. Fixed cost0
c. Undefined
d. Undefined

12. _____ are expenses whose total does not change in proportion to the activity of a business, within the relevant time period or scale of production
a. Fixed costs0
b. Thing
c. Undefined
d. Undefined

13. _____ is the change in total cost that arises when the quantity produced changes by one unit.
a. Marginal cost0
b. Thing
c. Undefined
d. Undefined

14. U.S. liquid _____ is legally defined as 231 cubic inches, and is equal to 3.785411784 litres or abotu 0.13368 cubic feet. This is the most common definition of a _____. The U.S. fluid ounce is defined as 1/128 of a U.S. _____.
a. Thing
b. Gallon0
c. Undefined
d. Undefined

15. _____ is a kind of property which exists as magnitude or multitude. It is among the basic classes of things along with quality, substance, change, and relation.
a. Thing
b. Amount0
c. Undefined
d. Undefined

16. _____ is a term used in accounting, economics and finance with reference to the fact that assets with finite lives lose value over time.
a. Depreciation0
b. Thing
c. Undefined
d. Undefined

17. In mathematics, a _____ is the result of multiplying, or an expression that identifies factors to be multiplied.
a. Thing
b. Product0
c. Undefined
d. Undefined

18. In geometry, two lines or planes if one falls on the other in such a way as to create congruent adjacent angles. The term may be used as a noun or adjective. Thus, referring to Figure 1, the line AB is the _____ to CD through the point B.
a. Thing
b. Perpendicular0
c. Undefined
d. Undefined

19. In astronomy, geography, geometry and related sciences and contexts, a plane is said to be _____ at a given point if it is locally perpendicular to the gradient of the gravity field, i.e., with the direction of the gravitational force at that point.
a. Horizontal0
b. Thing
c. Undefined
d. Undefined

20. A _____ is a set of numbers that designate location in a given reference system, such as x,y in a planar _____ system or an x,y,z in a three-dimensional _____ system.
a. Coordinate0
b. Thing
c. Undefined
d. Undefined

21. A _____ is a compensation which workers receive in exchange for their labor.
a. Wage0
b. Thing
c. Undefined
d. Undefined

22. A _____ is a quantity that denotes the proportional amount or magnitude of one quantity relative to another.
a. Ratio0
b. Thing
c. Undefined
d. Undefined

23. An _____ is a combination of numbers, operators, grouping symbols and/or free variables and bound variables arranged in a meaningful way which can be evaluated..
a. Thing
b. Expression0
c. Undefined
d. Undefined

24. In economics, supply and _____ describe market relations between prospective sellers and buyers of a good.
a. Thing
b. Demand0
c. Undefined
d. Undefined

25. In mathematics, the _____ of a coordinate system is the point where the axes of the system intersect.
a. Thing
b. Origin0
c. Undefined
d. Undefined

26. _____ is a relation in Euclidean geometry among the three sides of a right triangle.
a. Thing
b. Pythagorean Theorem0
c. Undefined
d. Undefined

27. In mathematics, a _____ is a statement that can be proved on the basis of explicitly stated or previously agreed assumptions.

Chapter 2. The Derivative

a. Theorem0
c. Undefined
b. Thing
d. Undefined

28. In mathematics, an _____, mean, or central tendency of a data set refers to a measure of the "middle" or "expected" value of the data set.
   a. Concept
   b. Average0
   c. Undefined
   d. Undefined

29. _____ is a synonym for information.
   a. Data0
   b. Thing
   c. Undefined
   d. Undefined

30. The word _____ comes from the Latin word linearis, which means created by lines.
   a. Linear0
   b. Thing
   c. Undefined
   d. Undefined

31. A _____ is a first degree polynomial mathematical function of the form: f(x) = mx + b where m and b are real constants and x is a real variable.
   a. Thing
   b. Linear function0
   c. Undefined
   d. Undefined

32. _____ is a business term for the amount of money that a company receives from its activities in a given period, mostly from sales of products and/or services to customers
   a. Revenue0
   b. Thing
   c. Undefined
   d. Undefined

33. The _____ is the United States federal government agency that collects taxes and enforces the internal revenue laws.
   a. Internal Revenue Service0
   b. Thing
   c. Undefined
   d. Undefined

34. The _____ is the total number of human beings alive on the planet Earth at a given time.
   a. World population0
   b. Thing
   c. Undefined
   d. Undefined

35. The population _____ is the total number of human beings alive on the planet Earth at a given time.
   a. Of the world0
   b. Thing
   c. Undefined
   d. Undefined

36. _____ is a way of expressing a number as a fraction of 100 per cent meaning "per hundred".
   a. Percent0
   b. Thing
   c. Undefined
   d. Undefined

37. In sociology and biology a _____ is the collection of people or organisms of a particular species living in a given geographic area or space, usually measured by a census.

Chapter 2. The Derivative

    a. Population0
    c. Undefined
    b. Thing
    d. Undefined

38. In mathematics, defined and _____ are used to explain whether or not expressions have meaningful, sensible, and unambiguous values.
    a. Undefined0
    c. Undefined
    b. Thing
    d. Undefined

39. In mathematics, a _____ is a constant multiplicative factor of a certain object. The object can be such things as a variable, a vector, a function, etc. For example, the _____ of $9x^2$ is 9.
    a. Coefficient0
    c. Undefined
    b. Thing
    d. Undefined

40. In trigonometry, the _____ is a function defined as $\tan x = \sin x / \cos x$. The function is so-named because it can be defined as the length of a certain segment of a _____ (in the geometric sense) to the unit circle. In plane geometry, a line is _____ to a curve, at some point, if both line and curve pass through the point with the same direction.
    a. Thing
    c. Undefined
    b. Tangent0
    d. Undefined

41. _____ has two distinct but etymologically-related meanings: one in geometry and one in trigonometry.
    a. Tangent line0
    c. Undefined
    b. Thing
    d. Undefined

42. In mathematics, the concept of a _____ tries to capture the intuitive idea of a geometrical one-dimensional and continuous object. A simple example is the circle.
    a. Curve0
    c. Undefined
    b. Thing
    d. Undefined

43. In mathematics, _____ are the intuitive idea of a geometrical one-dimensional and continuous object.
    a. Curves0
    c. Undefined
    b. Thing
    d. Undefined

44. In Euclidean geometry, a _____ is the set of all points in a plane at a fixed distance, called the radius, from a given point, the center.
    a. Thing
    c. Undefined
    b. Circle0
    d. Undefined

45. In business, particularly accounting, a _____ is the time intervals that the accounts, statement, payments, or other calculations cover.
    a. Thing
    c. Undefined
    b. Period0
    d. Undefined

46. In geographic information systems, a _____ comprises an entity with a geographic location, typically determined by points, arcs, or polygons. Carriageways and cadastres exemplify _____ data.

Chapter 2. The Derivative

a. Thing
b. Feature0
c. Undefined
d. Undefined

47. _____, from Latin meaning "to make progress", is defined in two different ways. Pure economic _____ is the increase in wealth that an investor has from making an investment, taking into consideration all costs associated with that investment including the opportunity cost of capital.
    a. Profit0
    b. Thing
    c. Undefined
    d. Undefined

48. _____ is the extra revenue that an additional unit of product will bring a firm. It can also be described as the change in total revenue/change in number of units sold.
    a. Marginal revenue0
    b. Thing
    c. Undefined
    d. Undefined

49. In mathematics and the mathematical sciences, a _____ is a fixed, but possibly unspecified, value. This is in contrast to a variable, which is not fixed.
    a. Thing
    b. Constant0
    c. Undefined
    d. Undefined

50. _____ is a function whose values do not vary and thus are constant.
    a. Constant function0
    b. Thing
    c. Undefined
    d. Undefined

51. _____ is a mathematical subject that includes the study of limits, derivatives, integrals, and power series and constitutes a major part of modern university curriculum.
    a. Thing
    b. Calculus0
    c. Undefined
    d. Undefined

52. _____ has many meanings, most of which simply .
    a. Power0
    b. Thing
    c. Undefined
    d. Undefined

53. _____ is a method for differentiating expressions involving exponentiation the power operation.
    a. Power rule0
    b. Thing
    c. Undefined
    d. Undefined

54. A _____ is a set of possible values that a variable can take on in order to satisfy a given set of conditions, which may include equations and inequalities.
    a. Solution set0
    b. Thing
    c. Undefined
    d. Undefined

55. _____ is a trigonometric function that is the reciprocal of cosine.
    a. Thing
    b. Secant0
    c. Undefined
    d. Undefined

56. _____ of a curve is a line that intersects two or more points on the curve.

Chapter 2. The Derivative

a. Thing
c. Undefined
b. Secant line0
d. Undefined

57. In mathematics, there are several meanings of _____ depending on the subject.
a. Thing
c. Undefined
b. Degree0
d. Undefined

58. A _____ is 360° or 2∂ radians.
a. Thing
c. Undefined
b. Turn0
d. Undefined

59. In mathematics, a _____ is the end result of a division problem. It can also be expressed as the number of times the divisor divides into the dividend.
a. Thing
c. Undefined
b. Quotient0
d. Undefined

60. The function difference divided by the point difference is known as the _____
a. Thing
c. Undefined
b. Difference quotient0
d. Undefined

61. _____ are the basic objects of study in graph theory. Informally speaking, a graph is a set of objects called points, nodes, or vertices connected by links called lines or edges.
a. Thing
c. Undefined
b. Graphs0
d. Undefined

62. A _____ is the part of a fraction that tells how many equal parts make up a whole, and which is used in the name of the fraction: "halves", "thirds", "fourths" or "quarters", "fifths" and so on.
a. Concept
c. Undefined
b. Denominator0
d. Undefined

63. In mathematics, a _____ is an expression that is constructed from one or more variables and constants, using only the operations of addition, subtraction, multiplication, and constant positive whole number exponents. is a _____. Note in particular that division by an expression containing a variable is not in general allowed in polynomials. [1]
a. Thing
c. Undefined
b. Polynomial0
d. Undefined

64. In mathematics, a _____ number is a number which can be expressed as a ratio of two integers. Non-integer _____ numbers (commonly called fractions) are usually written as the vulgar fraction a / b, where b is not zero.
a. Rational0
c. Undefined
b. Thing
d. Undefined

65. In mathematics, a _____ is any function which can be written as the ratio of two polynomial functions.
a. Thing
c. Undefined
b. Rational function0
d. Undefined

Chapter 2. The Derivative

66. A _____ is a numeral used to indicate a count. The most common use of the word today is to name the part of a fraction that tells the number or count of equal parts.
   a. Numerator0
   b. Thing
   c. Undefined
   d. Undefined

67. _____, a field in mathematics, is the study of how functions change when their inputs change. The primary object of study in _____ is the derivative.
   a. Thing
   b. Differential calculus0
   c. Undefined
   d. Undefined

68. _____ is the state of being greater than any finite number, however large.
   a. Infinity0
   b. Thing
   c. Undefined
   d. Undefined

69. The plus and _____ signs are mathematical symbols used to represent the notions of positive and negative as well as the operations of addition and subtraction.
   a. Thing
   b. Minus0
   c. Undefined
   d. Undefined

70. _____ are objects, characters, or other concrete representations of ideas, concepts, or other abstractions.
   a. Thing
   b. Symbols0
   c. Undefined
   d. Undefined

71. In mathematics, _____ is the decomposition of an object into a product of other objects, or factors, which when multiplied together give the original.
   a. Factoring0
   b. Thing
   c. Undefined
   d. Undefined

72. A _____ is a unit of length, usually used to measure distance, in a number of different systems, including Imperial units, United States customary units and Norwegian/Swedish mil. Its size can vary from system to system, but in each is between 1 and 10 kilometers. In contemporary English contexts _____ refers to either:
   a. Mile0
   b. Thing
   c. Undefined
   d. Undefined

73. A _____ function is a function for which, intuitively, small changes in the input result in small changes in the output.
   a. Continuous0
   b. Event
   c. Undefined
   d. Undefined

74. Continuous functions are of utmost importance in mathematics and applications. However, not all functions are continuous. If a function is not continuous at a point in its domain, one says that it has a _____ there. The set of all points of _____ of a function may be a discrete set, a dense set, or even the entire domain of the function.
   a. Discontinuity0
   b. Thing
   c. Undefined
   d. Undefined

Chapter 2. The Derivative

75. _____ is the application of tools and a processing medium to the transformation of raw materials into finished goods for sale.
   a. Thing
   b. Manufacturing0
   c. Undefined
   d. Undefined

76. In mathematics, science including computer science, linguistics and engineering, an _____ is, generally speaking, an independent variable or input to a function.
   a. Argument0
   b. Thing
   c. Undefined
   d. Undefined

77. In economics _____ means before deductions brutto, e.g. _____ domestic or national product, or _____ profit or income
   a. Gross0
   b. Thing
   c. Undefined
   d. Undefined

78. _____ is the portion of income that is the subject of taxation according to the laws that determine what is income and the taxation rate for that income.
   a. Thing
   b. Taxable income0
   c. Undefined
   d. Undefined

79. A _____ is the result of the addition of a set of numbers. The numbers may be natural numbers, complex numbers, matrices, or still more complicated objects. An infinite _____ is a subtle procedure known as a series.
   a. Thing
   b. Sum0
   c. Undefined
   d. Undefined

80. In calculus, the _____ in differentiation is a method of finding the derivative of a function that is the sum of two other functions for which derivatives exist.
   a. Sum Rule0
   b. Thing
   c. Undefined
   d. Undefined

81. In mathematics, the _____ is a conic section generated by the intersection of a right circular conical surface and a plane parallel to a generating straight line of that surface. It can also be defined as locus of points in a plane which are equidistant from a given point.
   a. Thing
   b. Parabola0
   c. Undefined
   d. Undefined

82. A _____ is a symbolic representation denoting a quantity or expression. It often represents an "unknown" quantity that has the potential to change.
   a. Variable0
   b. Thing
   c. Undefined
   d. Undefined

83. Mathematical _____ is used to represent ideas.
   a. Thing
   b. Notation0
   c. Undefined
   d. Undefined

Chapter 2. The Derivative

84. In mathematics, an _____ is any of the arguments, i.e. "inputs", to a function. Thus if we have a function f(x), then x is a _____.
    a. Thing
    b. Independent variable0
    c. Undefined
    d. Undefined

85. In mathematics, a _____ number (or a _____) is a natural number that has exactly two (distinct) natural number divisors, which are 1 and the _____ number itself.
    a. Thing
    b. Prime0
    c. Undefined
    d. Undefined

86. In elementary algebra, an _____ is a set that contains every real number between two indicated numbers and may contain the two numbers themselves.
    a. Thing
    b. Interval0
    c. Undefined
    d. Undefined

87. The _____, the average in everyday English, which is also called the arithmetic _____ (and is distinguished from the geometric _____ or harmonic _____). The average is also called the sample _____. The expected value of a random variable, which is also called the population _____.
    a. Mean0
    b. Thing
    c. Undefined
    d. Undefined

88. A frame of _____ is a particular perspective from which the universe is observed.
    a. Reference0
    b. Thing
    c. Undefined
    d. Undefined

89. In mathematics, the additive inverse, or _____ of a number n is the number that, when added to n, yields zero. The additive inverse of n is denoted −n. For example, 7 is −7, because 7 + (−7) = 0, and the additive inverse of −0.3 is 0.3, because −0.3 + 0.3 = 0.
    a. Thing
    b. Opposite0
    c. Undefined
    d. Undefined

90. _____ Any process by which a specified characteristic usually amplitude of the output of a device is prevented from exceeding a predetermined value.
    a. Thing
    b. Limiting0
    c. Undefined
    d. Undefined

91. In mathematics, the _____ of a number n is the number that, when added to n, yields zero. The _____ of n is denoted −n. For example, 7 is −7, because 7 + (−7) = 0, and the _____ of −0.3 is 0.3, because −0.3 + 0.3 = 0.
    a. Thing
    b. Additive inverse0
    c. Undefined
    d. Undefined

92. _____ of an object is its speed in a particular direction.
    a. Thing
    b. Velocity0
    c. Undefined
    d. Undefined

93. _____ is defined as the rate of change or derivative with respect to time of velocity.

Chapter 2. The Derivative

   a. Thing
   c. Undefined
   b. Acceleration0
   d. Undefined

94. _____ asserts that the maximum output of a technologically-determined production process is a mathematical function of input factors of production.
   a. Production function0
   c. Undefined
   b. Thing
   d. Undefined

95. A _____ fraction is a fraction in which the absolute value of the numerator is less than the denominator--hence, the absolute value of the fraction is less than 1.
   a. Proper0
   c. Undefined
   b. Thing
   d. Undefined

96. _____ is the transport of people on a trip/journey or the process or time involved in a person or object moving from one location to another.
   a. Travel0
   c. Undefined
   b. Thing
   d. Undefined

97. _____ is a physical property of a system that underlies the common notions of hot and cold; something that is hotter has the greater _____.
   a. Thing
   c. Undefined
   b. Temperature0
   d. Undefined

98. _____ are a measure of time.
   a. Thing
   c. Undefined
   b. Minutes0
   d. Undefined

99. In common philosophical language, a proposition or _____, is the content of an assertion, that is, it is true-or-false and defined by the meaning of a particular piece of language.
   a. Concept
   c. Undefined
   b. Statement0
   d. Undefined

100. Acid _____ ratio measures the ability of a company to use its near cash or quick assets to immediately extinguish its current liabilities.
   a. Test0
   c. Undefined
   b. Thing
   d. Undefined

101. _____ is the level of functional and/or metabolic efficiency of an organism at both the micro level.
   a. Thing
   c. Undefined
   b. Health0
   d. Undefined

102. In geometry, the _____ of an object is a point in some sense in the middle of the object.
   a. Center0
   c. Undefined
   b. Thing
   d. Undefined

Chapter 3. Applications of the Derivative

1. A _____ is an abstract model that uses mathematical language to describe the behavior of a system. Eykhoff defined a _____ as 'a representation of the essential aspects of an existing system which presents knowledge of that system in usable form'.
   a. Mathematical model0
   b. Thing
   c. Undefined
   d. Undefined

2. The _____ is a measurement of how a function changes when the values of its inputs change.
   a. Derivative0
   b. Thing
   c. Undefined
   d. Undefined

3. The mathematical concept of a _____ expresses the intuitive idea of deterministic dependence between two quantities, one of which is viewed as primary and the other as secondary. A _____ then is a way to associate a unique output for each input of a specified type, for example, a real number or an element of a given set.
   a. Function0
   b. Thing
   c. Undefined
   d. Undefined

4. _____ are the basic objects of study in graph theory. Informally speaking, a graph is a set of objects called points, nodes, or vertices connected by links called lines or edges.
   a. Graphs0
   b. Thing
   c. Undefined
   d. Undefined

5. _____ is the study of terms and their use — of words and compound words that are used in specific contexts.
   a. Thing
   b. Terminology0
   c. Undefined
   d. Undefined

6. In elementary algebra, an _____ is a set that contains every real number between two indicated numbers and may contain the two numbers themselves.
   a. Thing
   b. Interval0
   c. Undefined
   d. Undefined

7. An _____ or an extremal point is a point that belongs to the extremity of something.
   a. Thing
   b. Extreme point0
   c. Undefined
   d. Undefined

8. The _____ is the highest point in a certain portion of a graph.
   a. Relative maximum0
   b. Thing
   c. Undefined
   d. Undefined

9. The _____ is the lowest point in a certain portion of a graph.
   a. Relative minimum0
   b. Thing
   c. Undefined
   d. Undefined

10. In mathematics, a _____ of a k-place relation $L \subseteq X_1 \times ... \times X_k$ is one of the sets X_j, $1 \leq j \leq k$. In the special case where k = 2 and $L \subseteq X_1 \times X_2$ is a function $L : X_1 \rightarrow X_2$, it is conventional to refer to X_1 as the _____ of the function and to refer to X_2 as the codomain of the function.

a. Thing
b. Domain0
c. Undefined
d. Undefined

11. A _____ function is a function for which, intuitively, small changes in the input result in small changes in the output.
   a. Continuous0
   b. Event
   c. Undefined
   d. Undefined

12. In geometry, an _____ is a point at which a line segment or ray terminates.
   a. Thing
   b. Endpoint0
   c. Undefined
   d. Undefined

13. The term _____ refers to the largest and the smallest element of a set.
   a. Thing
   b. Extreme value0
   c. Undefined
   d. Undefined

14. In mathematics, maxima and minima, known collectively as extrema, are the largest value maximum or smallest value minimum, that a function takes in a point either within a given neighborhood local _____ or on the function domain in its entirety global _____.
   a. Thing
   b. Extremum0
   c. Undefined
   d. Undefined

15. In mathematics, the concept of a _____ tries to capture the intuitive idea of a geometrical one-dimensional and continuous object. A simple example is the circle.
   a. Thing
   b. Curve0
   c. Undefined
   d. Undefined

16. _____ is often used to describe the measurement of the steepness, incline, gradient, or grade of a straight line. The _____ is defined as the ratio of the "rise" divided by the "run" between two points on a line, or in other words, the ratio of the altitude change to the horizontal distance between any two points on the line.
   a. Thing
   b. Slope0
   c. Undefined
   d. Undefined

17. In geographic information systems, a _____ comprises an entity with a geographic location, typically determined by points, arcs, or polygons. Carriageways and cadastres exemplify _____ data.
   a. Thing
   b. Feature0
   c. Undefined
   d. Undefined

18. In economics _____ means before deductions brutto, e.g. _____ domestic or national product, or _____ profit or income
   a. Gross0
   b. Thing
   c. Undefined
   d. Undefined

19. A _____ is a special kind of ratio, indicating a relationship between two measurements with different units, such as miles to gallons or cents to pounds.

Chapter 3. Applications of the Derivative 31

   a. Rate0
   b. Thing
   c. Undefined
   d. Undefined

20. In mathematics, a _____ or rhodonea curve is a sinusoid plotted in polar coordinates.
   a. Thing
   b. Rose0
   c. Undefined
   d. Undefined

21. In sociology and biology a _____ is the collection of people or organisms of a particular species living in a given geographic area or space, usually measured by a census.
   a. Thing
   b. Population0
   c. Undefined
   d. Undefined

22. In mathematics, an inequality is a statement about the relative size or order of two objects. For example 14 > 10, or 14 is _____ 10.
   a. Greater than0
   b. Thing
   c. Undefined
   d. Undefined

23. _____ is a physical property of a system that underlies the common notions of hot and cold; something that is hotter has the greater _____.
   a. Thing
   b. Temperature0
   c. Undefined
   d. Undefined

24. The _____, the average in everyday English, which is also called the arithmetic _____ (and is distinguished from the geometric _____ or harmonic _____). The average is also called the sample _____. The expected value of a random variable, which is also called the population _____.
   a. Mean0
   b. Thing
   c. Undefined
   d. Undefined

25. The _____ of a mathematical object is its size: a property by which it can be larger or smaller than other objects of the same kind; in technical terms, an ordering of the class of objects to which it belongs.
   a. Magnitude0
   b. Thing
   c. Undefined
   d. Undefined

26. The word _____ means curving in or hollowed inward.
   a. Concavity0
   b. Thing
   c. Undefined
   d. Undefined

27. In trigonometry, the _____ is a function defined as $\tan x = \sin x / \cos x$. The function is so-named because it can be defined as the length of a certain segment of a _____ (in the geometric sense) to the unit circle. In plane geometry, a line is _____ to a curve, at some point, if both line and curve pass through the point with the same direction.
   a. Tangent0
   b. Thing
   c. Undefined
   d. Undefined

28. _____ has two distinct but etymologically-related meanings: one in geometry and one in trigonometry.

a. Tangent line0
b. Thing
c. Undefined
d. Undefined

29. In mathematics, the _____ f is the collection of all ordered pairs . In particular, graph means the graphical representation of this collection, in the form of a curve or surface, together with axes, etc. Graphing on a Cartesian plane is sometimes referred to as curve sketching.
   a. Thing
   b. Graph of a function0
   c. Undefined
   d. Undefined

30. _____ is a a point on a curve at which the tangent crosses the curve itself.
   a. Inflection point0
   b. Thing
   c. Undefined
   d. Undefined

31. In mathematics, defined and _____ are used to explain whether or not expressions have meaningful, sensible, and unambiguous values.
   a. Thing
   b. Undefined0
   c. Undefined
   d. Undefined

32. An _____ is a straight line or curve A to which another curve B approaches closer and closer as one moves along it. As one moves along B, the space between it and the _____ A becomes smaller and smaller, and can in fact be made as small as one could wish by going far enough along. A curve may or may not touch or cross its _____. In fact, the curve may intersect the _____ an infinite number of times.
   a. Thing
   b. Asymptote0
   c. Undefined
   d. Undefined

33. Any point where a graph makes contact with an coordinate axis is called an _____ of the graph
   a. Thing
   b. Intercept0
   c. Undefined
   d. Undefined

34. _____ is a test to determine if a relation or its graph is a function or not
   a. Vertical line test0
   b. Thing
   c. Undefined
   d. Undefined

35. Acid _____ ratio measures the ability of a company to use its near cash or quick assets to immediately extinguish its current liabilities.
   a. Thing
   b. Test0
   c. Undefined
   d. Undefined

36. In astronomy, geography, geometry and related sciences and contexts, a plane is said to be _____ at a given point if it is locally perpendicular to the gradient of the gravity field, i.e., with the direction of the gravitational force at that point.
   a. Horizontal0
   b. Thing
   c. Undefined
   d. Undefined

37. _____ is a straight line or curve A to which another curve B the one being studied approaches closer and closer as one moves along it.

a. Thing
b. Vertical asymptote0
c. Undefined
d. Undefined

38. In mathematics, an _____, mean, or central tendency of a data set refers to a measure of the "middle" or "expected" value of the data set.
a. Concept
b. Average0
c. Undefined
d. Undefined

39. In mathematics, a _____ is the result of multiplying, or an expression that identifies factors to be multiplied.
a. Product0
b. Thing
c. Undefined
d. Undefined

40. The _____ of measurement are a globally standardized and modernized form of the metric system.
a. Units0
b. Thing
c. Undefined
d. Undefined

41. _____ is the application of tools and a processing medium to the transformation of raw materials into finished goods for sale.
a. Manufacturing0
b. Thing
c. Undefined
d. Undefined

42. _____ is the flow of blood in the cardiovascular system.
a. Blood flow0
b. Thing
c. Undefined
d. Undefined

43. _____ the expected value of a random variable displays the average or central value of the variable. It is a summary value of the distribution of the variable.
a. Thing
b. Determining0
c. Undefined
d. Undefined

44. _____ are a measure of time.
a. Minutes0
b. Thing
c. Undefined
d. Undefined

45. In mathematics, a _____ is any one of several different types of functions, mappings, operations, or transformations.
a. Projection0
b. Thing
c. Undefined
d. Undefined

46. A _____ is an individual or household that purchases and uses goods and services generated within the economy.
a. Consumer0
b. Thing
c. Undefined
d. Undefined

47. _____ is a statistical time-series measure of a weighted average of prices of a specified set of goods and services purchased by consumers

a. Consumer price index0
b. Thing
c. Undefined
d. Undefined

48. The word _____ is used in a variety of ways in mathematics.
    a. Index0
    b. Thing
    c. Undefined
    d. Undefined

49. A _____ is a function that assigns a number to subsets of a given set.
    a. Thing
    b. Measure0
    c. Undefined
    d. Undefined

50. The _____ of a solid object is the three-dimensional concept of how much space it occupies, often quantified numerically.
    a. Thing
    b. Volume0
    c. Undefined
    d. Undefined

51. In vector calculus, the _____ of a scalar field is a vector field which points in the direction of the greatest rate of increase of the scalar field, and whose magnitude is the greatest rate of change.
    a. Gradient0
    b. Thing
    c. Undefined
    d. Undefined

52. _____ is the estimation of a physical quantity such as distance, energy, temperature, or time.
    a. Measurement0
    b. Thing
    c. Undefined
    d. Undefined

53. _____ is a business term for the amount of money that a company receives from its activities in a given period, mostly from sales of products and/or services to customers
    a. Revenue0
    b. Thing
    c. Undefined
    d. Undefined

54. _____ of an object is its speed in a particular direction.
    a. Thing
    b. Velocity0
    c. Undefined
    d. Undefined

55. In mathematics, _____ are the intuitive idea of a geometrical one-dimensional and continuous object.
    a. Curves0
    b. Thing
    c. Undefined
    d. Undefined

56. In a mathematical proof or a syllogism, a _____ is a statement that is the logical consequence of preceding statements.
    a. Concept
    b. Conclusion0
    c. Undefined
    d. Undefined

57. _____ is a kind of property which exists as magnitude or multitude. It is among the basic classes of things along with quality, substance, change, and relation.

a. Thing
b. Amount0
c. Undefined
d. Undefined

58. Graphing on a Cartesian plane is sometimes referred to as _____.
a. Thing
b. Curve sketching0
c. Undefined
d. Undefined

59. A _____ is a number that is less than zero.
a. Thing
b. Negative number0
c. Undefined
d. Undefined

60. A _____ is a polynomial function of the form f(x) = $ax^2 + bx + c$, where a, b, c are real numbers and a , 0.
a. Quadratic function0
b. Event
c. Undefined
d. Undefined

61. In mathematics, the _____ is a conic section generated by the intersection of a right circular conical surface and a plane parallel to a generating straight line of that surface. It can also be defined as locus of points in a plane which are equidistant from a given point.
a. Parabola0
b. Thing
c. Undefined
d. Undefined

62. An _____ is a combination of numbers, operators, grouping symbols and/or free variables and bound variables arranged in a meaningful way which can be evaluated..
a. Expression0
b. Thing
c. Undefined
d. Undefined

63. A _____ is a negotiable instrument instructing a financial institution to pay a specific amount of a specific currency from a specific demand account held in the maker/depositor's name with that institution. Both the maker and payee may be natural persons or legal entities.
a. Check0
b. Thing
c. Undefined
d. Undefined

64. In mathematics, _____ is the decomposition of an object into a product of other objects, or factors, which when multiplied together give the original.
a. Factoring0
b. Thing
c. Undefined
d. Undefined

65. In statistics, a _____ measure is one which is measuring what is supposed to measure.
a. Valid0
b. Thing
c. Undefined
d. Undefined

66. In mathematics, science including computer science, linguistics and engineering, an _____ is, generally speaking, an independent variable or input to a function.
a. Argument0
b. Thing
c. Undefined
d. Undefined

67. In mathematics, a _____ is an expression that is constructed from one or more variables and constants, using only the operations of addition, subtraction, multiplication, and constant positive whole number exponents. is a _____. Note in particular that division by an expression containing a variable is not in general allowed in polynomials. [1]
   a. Polynomial0
   b. Thing
   c. Undefined
   d. Undefined

68. A _____ is a set of numbers that designate location in a given reference system, such as x,y in a planar _____ system or an x,y,z in a three-dimensional _____ system.
   a. Coordinate0
   b. Thing
   c. Undefined
   d. Undefined

69. In linear algebra, the _____ of an n-by-n square matrix A is defined to be the sum of the elements on the main diagonal of A,
   a. Trace0
   b. Thing
   c. Undefined
   d. Undefined

70. The word _____ comes from the Latin word linearis, which means created by lines.
   a. Thing
   b. Linear0
   c. Undefined
   d. Undefined

71. A _____ is a first degree polynomial mathematical function of the form: f(x) = mx + b where m and b are real constants and x is a real variable.
   a. Linear function0
   b. Thing
   c. Undefined
   d. Undefined

72. _____ is the fee paid on borrowed money.
   a. Interest0
   b. Thing
   c. Undefined
   d. Undefined

73. A quadratic equation with real solutions, called roots, which may be real or complex, is given by the _____: $x = \frac{-b \pm \sqrt{b^2 - 4ac}}{2a}$.
   a. Thing
   b. Quadratic formula0
   c. Undefined
   d. Undefined

74. In Euclidean geometry, an _____ is a closed segment of a differentiable curve in the two-dimensional plane; for example, a circular _____ is a segment of a circle.
   a. Concept
   b. Arc0
   c. Undefined
   d. Undefined

75. The metre (or _____, see spelling differences) is a measure of length. It is the basic unit of length in the metric system and in the International System of Units (SI), used around the world for general and scientific purposes.
   a. Concept
   b. Meter0
   c. Undefined
   d. Undefined

76. _____, in a human resources context refers to the characteristic of a given company or industry, relative to rate at which an employer gains and loses staff.

Chapter 3. Applications of the Derivative 37

    a. Thing
    b. Turnover0
    c. Undefined
    d. Undefined

77. In business, particularly accounting, a _____ is the time intervals that the accounts, statement, payments, or other calculations cover.
    a. Thing
    b. Period0
    c. Undefined
    d. Undefined

78. In mathematics, a _____ is a countable collection of open covers of a topological space that satisfies certain separation axioms.
    a. Thing
    b. Development0
    c. Undefined
    d. Undefined

79. In computer science, an _____ is the problem of finding the best solution from all feasible solutions.
    a. Thing
    b. Optimization problem0
    c. Undefined
    d. Undefined

80. _____, from Latin meaning "to make progress", is defined in two different ways. Pure economic _____ is the increase in wealth that an investor has from making an investment, taking into consideration all costs associated with that investment including the opportunity cost of capital.
    a. Profit0
    b. Thing
    c. Undefined
    d. Undefined

81. _____ determines whether a given stationary point of a function is a maximum or a minimum.
    a. Second derivative test0
    b. Thing
    c. Undefined
    d. Undefined

82. A _____ is a simplified and structured visual representation of concepts, ideas, constructions, relations, statistical data, anatomy etc used in all aspects of human activities to visualize and clarify the topic.
    a. Diagram0
    b. Thing
    c. Undefined
    d. Undefined

83. A _____ is a symbolic representation denoting a quantity or expression. It often represents an "unknown" quantity that has the potential to change.
    a. Variable0
    b. Thing
    c. Undefined
    d. Undefined

84. In common philosophical language, a proposition or _____, is the content of an assertion, that is, it is true-or-false and defined by the meaning of a particular piece of language.
    a. Concept
    b. Statement0
    c. Undefined
    d. Undefined

85. In mathematics, a _____ is a condition that a solution to an optimization problem must satisfy in order to be acceptable.

a. Thing
b. Constraint0
c. Undefined
d. Undefined

86. In plane geometry, a _____ is a polygon with four equal sides, four right angles, and parallel opposite sides. In algebra, the _____ of a number is that number multiplied by itself.
   a. Thing
   b. Square0
   c. Undefined
   d. Undefined

87. In classical geometry, a _____ of a circle or sphere is any line segment from its center to its boundary. By extension, the _____ of a circle or sphere is the length of any such segment. The _____ is half the diameter. In science and engineering the term _____ of curvature is commonly used as a synonym for _____.
   a. Thing
   b. Radius0
   c. Undefined
   d. Undefined

88. In mathematics and the mathematical sciences, a _____ is a fixed, but possibly unspecified, value. This is in contrast to a variable, which is not fixed.
   a. Thing
   b. Constant0
   c. Undefined
   d. Undefined

89. _____ is the distance around a given two-dimensional object. As a general rule, the _____ of a polygon can always be calculated by adding all the length of the sides together. So, the formula for triangles is P = a + b + c, where a, b and c stand for each side of it. For quadrilaterals the equation is P = a + b + c + d. For equilateral polygons, P = na, where n is the number of sides and a is the side length.
   a. Perimeter0
   b. Thing
   c. Undefined
   d. Undefined

90. _____ is a set, with some particular properties and usually some additional structure, such as the operations of addition or multiplication, for instance.
   a. Thing
   b. Space0
   c. Undefined
   d. Undefined

91. In geometry, a _____ is defined as a quadrilateral where all four of its angles are right angles.
   a. Thing
   b. Rectangle0
   c. Undefined
   d. Undefined

92. A _____ is the result of the addition of a set of numbers. The numbers may be natural numbers, complex numbers, matrices, or still more complicated objects. An infinite _____ is a subtle procedure known as a series.
   a. Thing
   b. Sum0
   c. Undefined
   d. Undefined

93. A _____ is the part of the dividend that is left over when the dividend is not evenly divisible by the divisor.
   a. Thing
   b. Remainder0
   c. Undefined
   d. Undefined

94. In geometry, two lines or planes if one falls on the other in such a way as to create congruent adjacent angles. The term may be used as a noun or adjective. Thus, referring to Figure 1, the line AB is the _____ to CD through the point B.

Chapter 3. Applications of the Derivative 39

    a. Perpendicular0   b. Thing
    c. Undefined   d. Undefined

95. A _____ is a unit of length, usually used to measure distance, in a number of different systems, including Imperial units, United States customary units and Norwegian/Swedish mil. Its size can vary from system to system, but in each is between 1 and 10 kilometers. In contemporary English contexts _____ refers to either:
    a. Thing   b. Mile0
    c. Undefined   d. Undefined

96. _____ is a unit of speed, expressing the number of international miles covered per hour.
    a. Miles per hour0   b. Thing
    c. Undefined   d. Undefined

97. Compass and straightedge or ruler-and-compass _____ is the _____ of lengths or angles using only an idealized ruler and compass.
    a. Thing   b. Construction0
    c. Undefined   d. Undefined

98. In mathematics, the _____ of a coordinate system is the point where the axes of the system intersect.
    a. Thing   b. Origin0
    c. Undefined   d. Undefined

99. _____ is a list of goods and materials, or those goods and materials themselves, held available in stock by a business
    a. Thing   b. Inventory0
    c. Undefined   d. Undefined

100. Order theory is a branch of mathematics that studies various kinds of binary relations that capture the intuitive notion of a mathematical _____.
    a. Thing   b. Ordering0
    c. Undefined   d. Undefined

101. A _____ is a plan of action to guide decisions and actions.
    a. Thing   b. Policy0
    c. Undefined   d. Undefined

102. _____ is a model that defines the optimal quantity to order that minimizes total variable costs required to order and hold inventory.
    a. Economic order quantity0   b. Thing
    c. Undefined   d. Undefined

103. In mathematics, two quantities are called _____ if they vary in such a way that one of the quantities is a constant multiple of the other, or equivalently if they have a constant ratio.
    a. Proportional0   b. Thing
    c. Undefined   d. Undefined

104. In mathematics, a _____ of a number x is a number r such that r^2 = x, or in words, a number r whose square (the result of multiplying the number by itself) is x.
   a. Thing
   b. Square root0
   c. Undefined
   d. Undefined

105. In mathematics, a _____ of a complex-valued function f is a member x of the domain of f such that f(x) vanishes at x, that is, x : f (x) = 0.
   a. Thing
   b. Root0
   c. Undefined
   d. Undefined

106. In geometry, a _____ is the intersection of a body in 2-dimensional space with a line, or of a body in 3-dimensional space with a plane
   a. Cross section0
   b. Thing
   c. Undefined
   d. Undefined

107. _____ is the sub-discipline of fluid mechanics dealing with fluids liquids and gases in motion.
   a. Thing
   b. Fluid flow0
   c. Undefined
   d. Undefined

108. _____, in law and economics, is a form of risk management primarily used to hedge against the risk of a contingent loss.
   a. Insurance0
   b. Thing
   c. Undefined
   d. Undefined

109. _____ is the transport of people on a trip/journey or the process or time involved in a person or object moving from one location to another.
   a. Thing
   b. Travel0
   c. Undefined
   d. Undefined

110. Generally, a _____ is a splitting of something into parts.
   a. Thing
   b. Partition0
   c. Undefined
   d. Undefined

111. _____ is a synonym for information.
   a. Thing
   b. Data0
   c. Undefined
   d. Undefined

112. _____ is the property of a physical object that quantifies the amount of matter and energy it is equivalent to.
   a. Thing
   b. Mass0
   c. Undefined
   d. Undefined

113. _____ is a mathematical subject that includes the study of limits, derivatives, integrals, and power series and constitutes a major part of modern university curriculum.
   a. Calculus0
   b. Thing
   c. Undefined
   d. Undefined

Chapter 3. Applications of the Derivative 41

114. In geometry, the _____ of an object is a point in some sense in the middle of the object.
   a. Center0
   b. Thing
   c. Undefined
   d. Undefined

115. _____ is the change in total cost that arises when the quantity produced changes by one unit.
   a. Marginal cost0
   b. Thing
   c. Undefined
   d. Undefined

116. _____ is the extra revenue that an additional unit of product will bring a firm. It can also be described as the change in total revenue/change in number of units sold.
   a. Marginal revenue0
   b. Thing
   c. Undefined
   d. Undefined

117. In economics, supply and _____ describe market relations between prospective sellers and buyers of a good.
   a. Thing
   b. Demand0
   c. Undefined
   d. Undefined

118. _____ can be defined as the graph depicting the relationship between the price of a certain commodity, and the amount of it that consumers are willing and able to purchase at that given price demand.
   a. Thing
   b. Demand curve0
   c. Undefined
   d. Undefined

119. _____ are activities that are governed by a set of rules or customs and often engaged in competitively.
   a. Thing
   b. Sports0
   c. Undefined
   d. Undefined

120. Fixed costs are expenses whose total does not change in proportion to the activity of a business.Unit fixed costs decline with volume following a retangular hyperbola as the volume of production.Variable costs by contrast change in relation to the activity of a business such as sales or production volume.Along with variable costs,fixed costs make up one of the two components of total cost. In the most simple production function total cost is equal to fixed costs plus variable costs.In accounting terminology, fixed costs will broadly include all costs which are not included in cost of goods sold, and variable costs are those captured in costs of goods sold. The implicit assumption required to make the equivalence between the accounting and economics terminology is that the accounting period is equal to the period in which fixed costs do not vary in relation to production. In practice, this equivalence does not always hold and depending on the period under consideration by management, some overhead expenses can be adjusted by management, and the specific allocation of each expense to each category will be decided under cost accounting.In business planning and management accounting, usage of the terms fixed costs, variable costs and others will often differ from usage in economics, and may depend on the intended use. For example, costs may be segregated into per unit costs fixed costs per period, and variable costs as a proportion of revenue. Capital expenditures will usually be allocated separately, and depending on the purpose, a portion may be regularly allocated to expenses as depreciation and amortization and seen as a _____ per period, or the entire amount may be considered upfront fixed costs.
   a. Fixed cost0
   b. Thing
   c. Undefined
   d. Undefined

121. _____ are expenses whose total does not change in proportion to the activity of a business, within the relevant time period or scale of production

a. Fixed costs0
b. Thing
c. Undefined
d. Undefined

122. A _____ is a type of debt. All material things can be lent but this article focuses exclusively on monetary loans. Like all debt instruments, a _____ entails the redistribution of financial assets over time, between the lender and the borrower.
a. Loan0
b. Thing
c. Undefined
d. Undefined

123. _____ is the middle point of a line segment.
a. Thing
b. Midpoint0
c. Undefined
d. Undefined

124. A pair of angles is _____ if their respective measures sum to 180 degrees.
a. Concept
b. Supplementary0
c. Undefined
d. Undefined

125. _____ is a function whose values do not vary and thus are constant.
a. Constant function0
b. Thing
c. Undefined
d. Undefined

126. In finance, a _____ is collateral that the holder of a position in securities, options, or futures contracts has to deposit to cover the credit risk of his counterparty.
a. Margin0
b. Thing
c. Undefined
d. Undefined

Chapter 4. Techniques of Differentiation

1. In mathematics, a _____ is the result of multiplying, or an expression that identifies factors to be multiplied.
   - a. Thing
   - b. Product0
   - c. Undefined
   - d. Undefined

2. The _____ governs the differentiation of products of differentiable functions.
   - a. Thing
   - b. Product rule0
   - c. Undefined
   - d. Undefined

3. In mathematics, a _____ is the end result of a division problem. It can also be expressed as the number of times the divisor divides into the dividend.
   - a. Quotient0
   - b. Thing
   - c. Undefined
   - d. Undefined

4. The _____ is a method of finding the derivative of a function that is the quotient of two other functions for which derivatives exist.
   - a. Quotient rule0
   - b. Thing
   - c. Undefined
   - d. Undefined

5. In calculus, the _____ is a formula for the derivative of the composite of two functions.
   - a. Concept
   - b. Chain rule0
   - c. Undefined
   - d. Undefined

6. _____ has many meanings, most of which simply .
   - a. Thing
   - b. Power0
   - c. Undefined
   - d. Undefined

7. _____ is a method for differentiating expressions involving exponentiation the power operation.
   - a. Power rule0
   - b. Thing
   - c. Undefined
   - d. Undefined

8. A _____ is the result of the addition of a set of numbers. The numbers may be natural numbers, complex numbers, matrices, or still more complicated objects. An infinite _____ is a subtle procedure known as a series.
   - a. Thing
   - b. Sum0
   - c. Undefined
   - d. Undefined

9. In calculus, the _____ in differentiation is a method of finding the derivative of a function that is the sum of two other functions for which derivatives exist.
   - a. Sum Rule0
   - b. Thing
   - c. Undefined
   - d. Undefined

10. The _____ is a measurement of how a function changes when the values of its inputs change.
    - a. Thing
    - b. Derivative0
    - c. Undefined
    - d. Undefined

11. The mathematical concept of a _____ expresses the intuitive idea of deterministic dependence between two quantities, one of which is viewed as primary and the other as secondary. A _____ then is a way to associate a unique output for each input of a specified type, for example, a real number or an element of a given set.

a. Function0 b. Thing
c. Undefined d. Undefined

12. A _____ is a special kind of ratio, indicating a relationship between two measurements with different units, such as miles to gallons or cents to pounds.
    a. Thing b. Rate0
    c. Undefined d. Undefined

13. _____ is to give an equation R(x,y) = S(x,y) that at least in part has the same graph as y = f(x).
    a. Thing b. Implicit differentiation0
    c. Undefined d. Undefined

14. In differential calculus, _____ problems involve finding the rate at which a quantity is changing by relating that quantity to other quantities whose rates of change are known.
    a. Related rates0 b. Thing
    c. Undefined d. Undefined

15. _____, a field in mathematics, is the study of how functions change when their inputs change. The primary object of study in _____ is the derivative.
    a. Thing b. Differential calculus0
    c. Undefined d. Undefined

16. In mathematics, _____ expressions is used to reduce the expression into the lowest possible term.
    a. Thing b. Simplifying0
    c. Undefined d. Undefined

17. A _____ is a numeral used to indicate a count. The most common use of the word today is to name the part of a fraction that tells the number or count of equal parts.
    a. Numerator0 b. Thing
    c. Undefined d. Undefined

18. The plus and _____ signs are mathematical symbols used to represent the notions of positive and negative as well as the operations of addition and subtraction.
    a. Minus0 b. Thing
    c. Undefined d. Undefined

19. _____ are external two-dimensional outlines, with the appearance or configuration of some thing - in contrast to the matter or content or substance of which it is composed.
    a. Thing b. Shapes0
    c. Undefined d. Undefined

20. In mathematics, the concept of a _____ tries to capture the intuitive idea of a geometrical one-dimensional and continuous object. A simple example is the circle.
    a. Curve0 b. Thing
    c. Undefined d. Undefined

Chapter 4. Techniques of Differentiation

21. In mathematics, _____ are the intuitive idea of a geometrical one-dimensional and continuous object.
    a. Thing
    b. Curves0
    c. Undefined
    d. Undefined

22. In mathematics, an _____, mean, or central tendency of a data set refers to a measure of the "middle" or "expected" value of the data set.
    a. Concept
    b. Average0
    c. Undefined
    d. Undefined

23. _____ is the change in total cost that arises when the quantity produced changes by one unit.
    a. Marginal cost0
    b. Thing
    c. Undefined
    d. Undefined

24. A _____ function is a function for which, intuitively, small changes in the input result in small changes in the output.
    a. Continuous0
    b. Event
    c. Undefined
    d. Undefined

25. An _____ is a combination of numbers, operators, grouping symbols and/or free variables and bound variables arranged in a meaningful way which can be evaluated..
    a. Expression0
    b. Thing
    c. Undefined
    d. Undefined

26. In mathematics, _____ is the decomposition of an object into a product of other objects, or factors, which when multiplied together give the original.
    a. Factoring0
    b. Thing
    c. Undefined
    d. Undefined

27. In mathematics, a _____ is a statement that can be proved on the basis of explicitly stated or previously agreed assumptions.
    a. Theorem0
    b. Thing
    c. Undefined
    d. Undefined

28. In mathematics, science including computer science, linguistics and engineering, an _____ is, generally speaking, an independent variable or input to a function.
    a. Argument0
    b. Thing
    c. Undefined
    d. Undefined

29. _____ is a straight line or curve A to which another curve B the one being studied approaches closer and closer as one moves along it.
    a. Thing
    b. Vertical asymptote0
    c. Undefined
    d. Undefined

30. _____ are the basic objects of study in graph theory. Informally speaking, a graph is a set of objects called points, nodes, or vertices connected by links called lines or edges.

a. Graphs0
b. Thing
c. Undefined
d. Undefined

31. An _____ is a straight line or curve A to which another curve B approaches closer and closer as one moves along it. As one moves along B, the space between it and the _____ A becomes smaller and smaller, and can in fact be made as small as one could wish by going far enough along. A curve may or may not touch or cross its _____. In fact, the curve may intersect the _____ an infinite number of times.
   a. Thing
   b. Asymptote0
   c. Undefined
   d. Undefined

32. _____ means in succession or back-to-back
   a. Consecutive0
   b. Thing
   c. Undefined
   d. Undefined

33. In statistics, _____ means the most frequent value assumed by a random variable, or occurring in a sampling of a random variable.
   a. Concept
   b. Mode0
   c. Undefined
   d. Undefined

34. In geometry, a line _____ is a part of a line that is bounded by two end points, and contains every point on the line between its end points.
   a. Segment0
   b. Concept
   c. Undefined
   d. Undefined

35. A _____ is a part of a line that is bounded by two end points, and contains every point on the line between its end points.
   a. Line segment0
   b. Thing
   c. Undefined
   d. Undefined

36. In trigonometry, the _____ is a function defined as $\tan x = \sin x / \cos x$. The function is so-named because it can be defined as the length of a certain segment of a _____ (in the geometric sense) to the unit circle. In plane geometry, a line is _____ to a curve, at some point, if both line and curve pass through the point with the same direction.
   a. Thing
   b. Tangent0
   c. Undefined
   d. Undefined

37. _____ has two distinct but etymologically-related meanings: one in geometry and one in trigonometry.
   a. Tangent line0
   b. Thing
   c. Undefined
   d. Undefined

38. In astronomy, geography, geometry and related sciences and contexts, a plane is said to be _____ at a given point if it is locally perpendicular to the gradient of the gravity field, i.e., with the direction of the gravitational force at that point.
   a. Thing
   b. Horizontal0
   c. Undefined
   d. Undefined

Chapter 4. Techniques of Differentiation   47

39. _____ is often used to describe the measurement of the steepness, incline, gradient, or grade of a straight line. The _____ is defined as the ratio of the "rise" divided by the "run" between two points on a line, or in other words, the ratio of the altitude change to the horizontal distance between any two points on the line.
   a. Slope0
   b. Thing
   c. Undefined
   d. Undefined

40. In plane geometry, a _____ is a polygon with four equal sides, four right angles, and parallel opposite sides. In algebra, the _____ of a number is that number multiplied by itself.
   a. Square0
   b. Thing
   c. Undefined
   d. Undefined

41. The metre (or _____, see spelling differences) is a measure of length. It is the basic unit of length in the metric system and in the International System of Units (SI), used around the world for general and scientific purposes.
   a. Concept
   b. Meter0
   c. Undefined
   d. Undefined

42. The _____ of measurement are a globally standardized and modernized form of the metric system.
   a. Units0
   b. Thing
   c. Undefined
   d. Undefined

43. _____ is a business term for the amount of money that a company receives from its activities in a given period, mostly from sales of products and/or services to customers
   a. Revenue0
   b. Thing
   c. Undefined
   d. Undefined

44. _____ is the extra revenue that an additional unit of product will bring a firm. It can also be described as the change in total revenue/change in number of units sold.
   a. Thing
   b. Marginal revenue0
   c. Undefined
   d. Undefined

45. _____ is the transport of people on a trip/journey or the process or time involved in a person or object moving from one location to another.
   a. Thing
   b. Travel0
   c. Undefined
   d. Undefined

46. A _____ is a unit of length, usually used to measure distance, in a number of different systems, including Imperial units, United States customary units and Norwegian/Swedish mil. Its size can vary from system to system, but in each is between 1 and 10 kilometers. In contemporary English contexts _____ refers to either:
   a. Mile0
   b. Thing
   c. Undefined
   d. Undefined

47. _____ of an object is its speed in a particular direction.
   a. Thing
   b. Velocity0
   c. Undefined
   d. Undefined

48. In geometry, a _____ is defined as a quadrilateral where all four of its angles are right angles.

a. Rectangle0 b. Thing
c. Undefined d. Undefined

49. _____ is a kind of property which exists as magnitude or multitude. It is among the basic classes of things along with quality, substance, change, and relation.
a. Amount0 b. Thing
c. Undefined d. Undefined

50. _____ is a way of expressing a number as a fraction of 100 per cent meaning "per hundred".
a. Percent0 b. Thing
c. Undefined d. Undefined

51. In sociology and biology a _____ is the collection of people or organisms of a particular species living in a given geographic area or space, usually measured by a census.
a. Population0 b. Thing
c. Undefined d. Undefined

52. U.S. liquid _____ is legally defined as 231 cubic inches, and is equal to 3.785411784 litres or abotu 0.13368 cubic feet. This is the most common definition of a _____. The U.S. fluid ounce is defined as 1/128 of a U.S. _____.
a. Thing b. Gallon0
c. Undefined d. Undefined

53. A _____ is a set of numbers that designate location in a given reference system, such as x,y in a planar _____ system or an x,y,z in a three-dimensional _____ system.
a. Thing b. Coordinate0
c. Undefined d. Undefined

54. A _____ is a quantity that denotes the proportional amount or magnitude of one quantity relative to another.
a. Thing b. Ratio0
c. Undefined d. Undefined

55. The word _____ is used in a variety of ways in mathematics.
a. Index0 b. Thing
c. Undefined d. Undefined

56. _____ is the property of a physical object that quantifies the amount of matter and energy it is equivalent to.
a. Mass0 b. Thing
c. Undefined d. Undefined

57. _____ is a statistical measure of the weight of a person scaled according to height. It was invented between 1830 and 1850 by the Belgian polymath Adolphe Quetelet during the course of developing "social physics".
a. Thing b. Body mass index0
c. Undefined d. Undefined

Chapter 4. Techniques of Differentiation

58. The _____ or kilogramme is the SI base unit of mass. It is defined as being equal to the mass of the international prototype of the _____.
   a. Kilogram0
   b. Thing
   c. Undefined
   d. Undefined

59. _____ is electromagnetic radiation with a wavelength that is visible to the eye (visible _____) or, in a technical or scientific context, electromagnetic radiation of any wavelength.
   a. Thing
   b. Light0
   c. Undefined
   d. Undefined

60. A _____ number is a positive integer which has a positive divisor other than one or itself.
   a. Thing
   b. Composite0
   c. Undefined
   d. Undefined

61. A _____, formed by the composition of one function on another, represents the application of the former to the result of the application of the latter to the argument of the composite.
   a. Composite function0
   b. Thing
   c. Undefined
   d. Undefined

62. In mathematics, a _____ of a number x is a number r such that $r^2 = x$, or in words, a number r whose square (the result of multiplying the number by itself) is x.
   a. Thing
   b. Square root0
   c. Undefined
   d. Undefined

63. In mathematics, a _____ of a complex-valued function f is a member x of the domain of f such that f(x) vanishes at x, that is, x : f (x) = 0.
   a. Thing
   b. Root0
   c. Undefined
   d. Undefined

64. In mathematics and the mathematical sciences, a _____ is a fixed, but possibly unspecified, value. This is in contrast to a variable, which is not fixed.
   a. Thing
   b. Constant0
   c. Undefined
   d. Undefined

65. A _____ is a symbolic representation denoting a quantity or expression. It often represents an "unknown" quantity that has the potential to change.
   a. Thing
   b. Variable0
   c. Undefined
   d. Undefined

66. In mathematics, a _____ of a positive integer n is a way of writing n as a sum of positive integers.
   a. Composition0
   b. Thing
   c. Undefined
   d. Undefined

67. In a mathematical proof or a syllogism, a _____ is a statement that is the logical consequence of preceding statements.

a. Concept
b. Conclusion0
c. Undefined
d. Undefined

68. A _____ is the part of a fraction that tells how many equal parts make up a whole, and which is used in the name of the fraction: "halves", "thirds", "fourths" or "quarters", "fifths" and so on.
    a. Concept
    b. Denominator0
    c. Undefined
    d. Undefined

69. The _____ is the lowest point in a certain portion of a graph.
    a. Relative minimum0
    b. Thing
    c. Undefined
    d. Undefined

70. A _____ is a three-dimensional solid object bounded by six square faces, facets, or sides, with three meeting at each vertex.
    a. Thing
    b. Cube0
    c. Undefined
    d. Undefined

71. The _____ of a solid object is the three-dimensional concept of how much space it occupies, often quantified numerically.
    a. Volume0
    b. Thing
    c. Undefined
    d. Undefined

72. _____ is the application of tools and a processing medium to the transformation of raw materials into finished goods for sale.
    a. Thing
    b. Manufacturing0
    c. Undefined
    d. Undefined

73. _____, from Latin meaning "to make progress", is defined in two different ways. Pure economic _____ is the increase in wealth that an investor has from making an investment, taking into consideration all costs associated with that investment including the opportunity cost of capital.
    a. Profit0
    b. Thing
    c. Undefined
    d. Undefined

74. In Euclidean geometry, a uniform _____ is a linear transformation that enlargers or diminishes objects, and whose _____ factor is the same in all directions. This is also called homothethy.
    a. Thing
    b. Scale0
    c. Undefined
    d. Undefined

75. _____ is a test to determine if a relation or its graph is a function or not
    a. Vertical line test0
    b. Thing
    c. Undefined
    d. Undefined

76. In mathematics, the _____ f is the collection of all ordered pairs . In particular, graph means the graphical representation of this collection, in the form of a curve or surface, together with axes, etc. Graphing on a Cartesian plane is sometimes referred to as curve sketching.

Chapter 4. Techniques of Differentiation

    a. Thing
    c. Undefined
    b. Graph of a function0
    d. Undefined

77. Acd _____ ratio measures the ability of a company to use its near cash or quick assets to immediately extinguish its current liabilities.
    a. Thing
    c. Undefined
    b. Test0
    d. Undefined

78. In mathematics, defined and _____ are used to explain whether or not expressions have meaningful, sensible, and unambiguous values.
    a. Thing
    c. Undefined
    b. Undefined0
    d. Undefined

79. In economics, an _____ is a contour line drawn through the set of points at which the same quantity of output is produced while changing the quantities of two or more inputs.
    a. Thing
    c. Undefined
    b. Isoquant0
    d. Undefined

80. _____ is the study of terms and their use — of words and compound words that are used in specific contexts.
    a. Terminology0
    c. Undefined
    b. Thing
    d. Undefined

81. In mathematics, the _____ (or modulus) of a real number is its numerical value without regard to its sign.
    a. Thing
    c. Undefined
    b. Absolute value0
    d. Undefined

82. In economics, supply and _____ describe market relations between prospective sellers and buyers of a good.
    a. Demand0
    c. Undefined
    b. Thing
    d. Undefined

83. In mathematics, an _____ is any of the arguments, i.e. "inputs", to a function. Thus if we have a function f(x), then x is a _____.
    a. Thing
    c. Undefined
    b. Independent variable0
    d. Undefined

84. In mathematics, the _____ of Bernoulli is an eight-shaped algebraic curve described by a Cartesian equation
    a. Lemniscate0
    c. Undefined
    b. Thing
    d. Undefined

85. An _____ of a product of sums expresses it as a sum of products by using the fact that multiplication distributes over addition.
    a. Thing
    c. Undefined
    b. Expansion0
    d. Undefined

Chapter 4. Techniques of Differentiation

86. In geometry, a _____ (Greek words diairo = divide and metro = measure) of a circle is any straight line segment that passes through the centre and whose endpoints are on the circular boundary, or, in more modern usage, the length of such a line segment. When using the word in the more modern sense, one speaks of the _____ rather than a _____, because all diameters of a circle have the same length. This length is twice the radius. The _____ of a circle is also the longest chord that the circle has.
   a. Thing
   b. Diameter0
   c. Undefined
   d. Undefined

87. _____ is a relation in Euclidean geometry among the three sides of a right triangle.
   a. Pythagorean Theorem0
   b. Thing
   c. Undefined
   d. Undefined

88. A pair of angles is _____ if their respective measures sum to 180 degrees.
   a. Supplementary0
   b. Concept
   c. Undefined
   d. Undefined

89. _____ is a particular type of curve: a hypocycloid with four cusps.
   a. Astroid0
   b. Thing
   c. Undefined
   d. Undefined

90. _____ was a highly influential French philosopher, mathematician, scientist, and writer. Dubbed the "Founder of Modern Philosophy", and the "Father of Modern Mathematics". His theories provided the basis for the calculus of Newton and Leibniz, by applying infinitesimal calculus to the tangent line problem, thus permitting the evolution of that branch of modern mathematics
   a. Person
   b. Descartes0
   c. Undefined
   d. Undefined

91. In classical geometry, a _____ of a circle or sphere is any line segment from its center to its boundary. By extension, the _____ of a circle or sphere is the length of any such segment. The _____ is half the diameter. In science and engineering the term _____ of curvature is commonly used as a synonym for _____.
   a. Radius0
   b. Thing
   c. Undefined
   d. Undefined

Chapter 5. Logarithm Functions

1. In mathematics, two quantities are called _____ if they vary in such a way that one of the quantities is a constant multiple of the other, or equivalently if they have a constant ratio.
   - a. Thing
   - b. Proportional0
   - c. Undefined
   - d. Undefined

2. A _____ is a special kind of ratio, indicating a relationship between two measurements with different units, such as miles to gallons or cents to pounds.
   - a. Thing
   - b. Rate0
   - c. Undefined
   - d. Undefined

3. _____ or investing is a term with several closely-related meanings in business management, finance and economics, related to saving or deferring consumption.
   - a. Thing
   - b. Investment0
   - c. Undefined
   - d. Undefined

4. _____ is a kind of property which exists as magnitude or multitude. It is among the basic classes of things along with quality, substance, change, and relation.
   - a. Thing
   - b. Amount0
   - c. Undefined
   - d. Undefined

5. _____ is the logarithm to the base e, where e is an irrational constant approximately equal to 2.718281828459.
   - a. Natural logarithm0
   - b. Thing
   - c. Undefined
   - d. Undefined

6. In mathematics, _____ growth occurs when the growth rate of a function is always proportional to the function's current size.
   - a. Exponential0
   - b. Thing
   - c. Undefined
   - d. Undefined

7. _____ is a decrease that follows an exponential function.
   - a. Exponential decay0
   - b. Thing
   - c. Undefined
   - d. Undefined

8. _____ is one of the most important functions in mathematics. A function commonly used to study growth and decay
   - a. Thing
   - b. Exponential function0
   - c. Undefined
   - d. Undefined

9. In mathematics, _____ occurs when the growth rate of a function is always proportional to the function's current size.
   - a. Thing
   - b. Exponential growth0
   - c. Undefined
   - d. Undefined

10. In mathematics, a _____ of a number x is the exponent y of the power by such that $x = b^y$. The value used for the base b must be neither 0 nor 1, nor a root of 1 in the case of the extension to complex numbers, and is typically 10, e, or 2.

a. Thing
b. Logarithm0
c. Undefined
d. Undefined

11. The mathematical concept of a _____ expresses the intuitive idea of deterministic dependence between two quantities, one of which is viewed as primary and the other as secondary. A _____ then is a way to associate a unique output for each input of a specified type, for example, a real number or an element of a given set.
   a. Function0
   b. Thing
   c. Undefined
   d. Undefined

12. In mathematics, the _____ of a function is the set of all "output" values produced by that function. Given a function $f : A \to B$, the _____ of f, is defined to be the set $\{x \in B : x = f(a) \text{ for some } a \in A\}$.
   a. Range0
   b. Thing
   c. Undefined
   d. Undefined

13. _____ is the level of functional and/or metabolic efficiency of an organism at both the micro level.
   a. Health0
   b. Thing
   c. Undefined
   d. Undefined

14. A _____ is a symbolic representation denoting a quantity or expression. It often represents an "unknown" quantity that has the potential to change.
   a. Variable0
   b. Thing
   c. Undefined
   d. Undefined

15. In mathematics, a _____ number is a number which can be expressed as a ratio of two integers. Non-integer _____ numbers (commonly called fractions) are usually written as the vulgar fraction a / b, where b is not zero.
   a. Rational0
   b. Thing
   c. Undefined
   d. Undefined

16. A _____ is a numeral used to indicate a count. The most common use of the word today is to name the part of a fraction that tells the number or count of equal parts.
   a. Thing
   b. Numerator0
   c. Undefined
   d. Undefined

17. _____, either of the curved-bracket punctuation marks that together make a set of _____
   a. Thing
   b. Parentheses0
   c. Undefined
   d. Undefined

18. _____ has many meanings, most of which simply .
   a. Thing
   b. Power0
   c. Undefined
   d. Undefined

19. In mathematics, the concept of a _____ tries to capture the intuitive idea of a geometrical one-dimensional and continuous object. A simple example is the circle.
   a. Thing
   b. Curve0
   c. Undefined
   d. Undefined

Chapter 5. Logarithm Functions

20. _____ are the basic objects of study in graph theory. Informally speaking, a graph is a set of objects called points, nodes, or vertices connected by links called lines or edges.
    a. Thing
    b. Graphs0
    c. Undefined
    d. Undefined

21. _____ is often used to describe the measurement of the steepness, incline, gradient, or grade of a straight line. The _____ is defined as the ratio of the "rise" divided by the "run" between two points on a line, or in other words, the ratio of the altitude change to the horizontal distance between any two points on the line.
    a. Thing
    b. Slope0
    c. Undefined
    d. Undefined

22. In astronomy, geography, geometry and related sciences and contexts, a plane is said to be _____ at a given point if it is locally perpendicular to the gradient of the gravity field, i.e., with the direction of the gravitational force at that point.
    a. Horizontal0
    b. Thing
    c. Undefined
    d. Undefined

23. _____ traditionally refers to the statistical process of determining comparable scores on different forms of an exam
    a. Equating0
    b. Thing
    c. Undefined
    d. Undefined

24. _____ is a mathematical operation, written a^n, involving two numbers, the base a and the exponent n.
    a. Exponentiating0
    b. Thing
    c. Undefined
    d. Undefined

25. _____ is a mathematical operation, written a^n, involving two numbers, the base a and the exponent n.
    a. Exponentiation0
    b. Thing
    c. Undefined
    d. Undefined

26. In mathematics and the mathematical sciences, a _____ is a fixed, but possibly unspecified, value. This is in contrast to a variable, which is not fixed.
    a. Thing
    b. Constant0
    c. Undefined
    d. Undefined

27. A _____ is 360° or 2∂ radians.
    a. Turn0
    b. Thing
    c. Undefined
    d. Undefined

28. A _____ is a deliberate process for transforming one or more inputs into one or more results.
    a. Thing
    b. Calculation0
    c. Undefined
    d. Undefined

29. _____ is a trigonometric function that is the reciprocal of cosine.
    a. Thing
    b. Secant0
    c. Undefined
    d. Undefined

30. _____ of a curve is a line that intersects two or more points on the curve.
    a. Thing
    b. Secant line0
    c. Undefined
    d. Undefined

31. The _____ is a measurement of how a function changes when the values of its inputs change.
    a. Derivative0
    b. Thing
    c. Undefined
    d. Undefined

32. In trigonometry, the _____ is a function defined as $\tan x = \sin x / \cos x$. The function is so-named because it can be defined as the length of a certain segment of a _____ (in the geometric sense) to the unit circle. In plane geometry, a line is _____ to a curve, at some point, if both line and curve pass through the point with the same direction.
    a. Thing
    b. Tangent0
    c. Undefined
    d. Undefined

33. _____ has two distinct but etymologically-related meanings: one in geometry and one in trigonometry.
    a. Thing
    b. Tangent line0
    c. Undefined
    d. Undefined

34. A _____ is a unit of length in the metric system, equal to one thousand metres, the current SI base unit of length
    a. Kilometer0
    b. Thing
    c. Undefined
    d. Undefined

35. In plane geometry, a _____ is a polygon with four equal sides, four right angles, and parallel opposite sides. In algebra, the _____ of a number is that number multiplied by itself.
    a. Square0
    b. Thing
    c. Undefined
    d. Undefined

36. In geometry, an _____ of a triangle is a straight line through a vertex and perpendicular to (i.e. forming a right angle with) the opposite side or an extension of the opposite side.
    a. Concept
    b. Altitude0
    c. Undefined
    d. Undefined

37. _____, a field in mathematics, is the study of how functions change when their inputs change. The primary object of study in _____ is the derivative.
    a. Differential calculus0
    b. Thing
    c. Undefined
    d. Undefined

38. The _____ of measurement are a globally standardized and modernized form of the metric system.
    a. Thing
    b. Units0
    c. Undefined
    d. Undefined

39. In calculus, the _____ is a formula for the derivative of the composite of two functions.
    a. Concept
    b. Chain rule0
    c. Undefined
    d. Undefined

40. A _____ is traditionally an infinitesimally small change in a variable.

Chapter 5. Logarithm Functions

    a. Thing
    c. Undefined
    b. Differential0
    d. Undefined

41. A _____ is a mathematical equation for an unknown function of one or several variables which relates the values of the function itself and of its derivatives of various orders.
    - a. Thing
    - b. Differential equation0
    - c. Undefined
    - d. Undefined

42. An _____ is a straight line or curve A to which another curve B approaches closer and closer as one moves along it. As one moves along B, the space between it and the _____ A becomes smaller and smaller, and can in fact be made as small as one could wish by going far enough along. A curve may or may not touch or cross its _____. In fact, the curve may intersect the _____ an infinite number of times.
    - a. Thing
    - b. Asymptote0
    - c. Undefined
    - d. Undefined

43. The _____ is the highest point in a certain portion of a graph.
    - a. Relative maximum0
    - b. Thing
    - c. Undefined
    - d. Undefined

44. _____ of an object is its speed in a particular direction.
    - a. Velocity0
    - b. Thing
    - c. Undefined
    - d. Undefined

45. _____ is defined as the rate of change or derivative with respect to time of velocity.
    - a. Acceleration0
    - b. Thing
    - c. Undefined
    - d. Undefined

46. _____ is a function whose values do not vary and thus are constant.
    - a. Constant function0
    - b. Thing
    - c. Undefined
    - d. Undefined

47. _____ is a method for differentiating expressions involving exponentiation the power operation.
    - a. Thing
    - b. Power rule0
    - c. Undefined
    - d. Undefined

48. _____ is a special mathematical relationship between two quantities.Two quantities are called proportional if they vary in such a way that one of the quantities is a constant multiple of the other, or equivalently if they have a constant ratio.
    - a. Proportionality0
    - b. Thing
    - c. Undefined
    - d. Undefined

49. In mathematics, a _____ (also spelled reflexion) is a map that transforms an object into its mirror image.
    - a. Reflection0
    - b. Concept
    - c. Undefined
    - d. Undefined

Chapter 5. Logarithm Functions

50. In mathematics, a _____ is a countable collection of open covers of a topological space that satisfies certain separation axioms.
    a. Development0
    b. Thing
    c. Undefined
    d. Undefined

51. In mathematics, _____ is a part of the set theoretic notion of function.
    a. Image0
    b. Thing
    c. Undefined
    d. Undefined

52. In mathematics, an inequality is a statement about the relative size or order of two objects. For example 14 > 10, or 14 is _____ 10.
    a. Thing
    b. Greater than0
    c. Undefined
    d. Undefined

53. An _____ is an equality that remains true regardless of the values of any variables that appear within it, to distinguish it from an equality which is true under more particular conditions.
    a. Identity0
    b. Thing
    c. Undefined
    d. Undefined

54. _____ element of an element x with respect to a binary operation * with identity element e is an element y such that x * y = y * x = e. In particular,
    a. Thing
    b. Inverse0
    c. Undefined
    d. Undefined

55. In mathematics, the _____ f is the collection of all ordered pairs . In particular, graph means the graphical representation of this collection, in the form of a curve or surface, together with axes, etc. Graphing on a Cartesian plane is sometimes referred to as curve sketching.
    a. Graph of a function0
    b. Thing
    c. Undefined
    d. Undefined

56. In mathematics, the _____ is the logarithm with base 10.
    a. Thing
    b. Common logarithm0
    c. Undefined
    d. Undefined

57. In mathematics, _____ expressions is used to reduce the expression into the lowest possible term.
    a. Simplifying0
    b. Thing
    c. Undefined
    d. Undefined

58. _____ or arithmetics is the oldest and most elementary branch of mathematics, used by almost everyone, for tasks ranging from simple daily counting to advanced science and business calculations.
    a. Arithmetic0
    b. Thing
    c. Undefined
    d. Undefined

59. _____ is a branch of mathematics concerning the study of structure, relation and quantity.

Chapter 5. Logarithm Functions

  a. Algebra0
  c. Undefined
  b. Concept
  d. Undefined

60. A _____ of a number is the product of that number with any integer.
  a. Thing
  c. Undefined
  b. Multiple0
  d. Undefined

61. _____ is a process of combining or accumulating. It may also refer to:
  a. Integration0
  c. Undefined
  b. Thing
  d. Undefined

62. _____ is a mathematical subject that includes the study of limits, derivatives, integrals, and power series and constitutes a major part of modern university curriculum.
  a. Thing
  c. Undefined
  b. Calculus0
  d. Undefined

63. A _____ is a set of numbers that designate location in a given reference system, such as x,y in a planar _____ system or an x,y,z in a three-dimensional _____ system.
  a. Thing
  c. Undefined
  b. Coordinate0
  d. Undefined

64. A _____ is the quantity that defines certain relatively constant characteristics of systems or functions..
  a. Thing
  c. Undefined
  b. Parameter0
  d. Undefined

65. In linear algebra, the _____ of an n-by-n square matrix A is defined to be the sum of the elements on the main diagonal of A,
  a. Trace0
  c. Undefined
  b. Thing
  d. Undefined

66. In mathematics, the _____ of two sets A and B is the set that contains all elements of A that also belong to B (or equivalently, all elements of B that also belong to A), but no other elements.
  a. Intersection0
  c. Undefined
  b. Thing
  d. Undefined

67. In mathematics, a _____ is the result of multiplying, or an expression that identifies factors to be multiplied.
  a. Product0
  c. Undefined
  b. Thing
  d. Undefined

68. The _____ governs the differentiation of products of differentiable functions.
  a. Thing
  c. Undefined
  b. Product rule0
  d. Undefined

69. In mathematics, a _____ is the end result of a division problem. It can also be expressed as the number of times the divisor divides into the dividend.

Chapter 5. Logarithm Functions

a. Quotient0
b. Thing
c. Undefined
d. Undefined

70. The _____ is a method of finding the derivative of a function that is the quotient of two other functions for which derivatives exist.
    a. Thing
    b. Quotient rule0
    c. Undefined
    d. Undefined

71. An _____ or an extremal point is a point that belongs to the extremity of something.
    a. Thing
    b. Extreme point0
    c. Undefined
    d. Undefined

72. The _____ is the lowest point in a certain portion of a graph.
    a. Thing
    b. Relative minimum0
    c. Undefined
    d. Undefined

73. _____, from Latin meaning "to make progress", is defined in two different ways. Pure economic _____ is the increase in wealth that an investor has from making an investment, taking into consideration all costs associated with that investment including the opportunity cost of capital.
    a. Thing
    b. Profit0
    c. Undefined
    d. Undefined

74. A _____ consists of one quarter of the coordinate plane.
    a. Quadrant0
    b. Thing
    c. Undefined
    d. Undefined

75. In geometry, a _____ is defined as a quadrilateral where all four of its angles are right angles.
    a. Rectangle0
    b. Thing
    c. Undefined
    d. Undefined

76. An _____ is when two lines intersect somewhere on a plane creating a right angle at intersection
    a. Axes0
    b. Thing
    c. Undefined
    d. Undefined

77. In mathematics, the _____ of a coordinate system is the point where the axes of the system intersect.
    a. Origin0
    b. Thing
    c. Undefined
    d. Undefined

78. Acid _____ ratio measures the ability of a company to use its near cash or quick assets to immediately extinguish its current liabilities.
    a. Test0
    b. Thing
    c. Undefined
    d. Undefined

79. _____ are a measure of time.

Chapter 5. Logarithm Functions

a. Thing
c. Undefined
b. Minutes0
d. Undefined

80. _____ is a way of expressing a number as a fraction of 100 per cent meaning "per hundred".
a. Percent0
c. Undefined
b. Thing
d. Undefined

81. A central concept in science and the scientific method is that all evidence must be _____, or empirically based, that is, dependent on evidence or consequences that are observable by the senses.
a. Thing
c. Undefined
b. Empirical0
d. Undefined

82. _____ is a synonym for information.
a. Data0
c. Undefined
b. Thing
d. Undefined

83. A _____ is a function that assigns a number to subsets of a given set.
a. Thing
c. Undefined
b. Measure0
d. Undefined

84. In epidemiology, an _____ is a disease that appears as new cases in a given human population, during a given period, at a rate that substantially exceeds with is "expected," based on recent experience.
a. Thing
c. Undefined
b. Epidemic0
d. Undefined

85. In sociology and biology a _____ is the collection of people or organisms of a particular species living in a given geographic area or space, usually measured by a census.
a. Thing
c. Undefined
b. Population0
d. Undefined

86. A _____ is the result of the addition of a set of numbers. The numbers may be natural numbers, complex numbers, matrices, or still more complicated objects. An infinite _____ is a subtle procedure known as a series.
a. Thing
c. Undefined
b. Sum0
d. Undefined

87. In geographic information systems, a _____ comprises an entity with a geographic location, typically determined by points, arcs, or polygons. Carriageways and cadastres exemplify _____ data.
a. Feature0
c. Undefined
b. Thing
d. Undefined

Chapter 6. Applications of the Exponential and Natural Logarithm Functions

1. _____ is the logarithm to the base e, where e is an irrational constant approximately equal to 2.718281828459.
   a. Natural logarithm0
   b. Thing
   c. Undefined
   d. Undefined

2. In mathematics, _____ growth occurs when the growth rate of a function is always proportional to the function's current size.
   a. Exponential0
   b. Thing
   c. Undefined
   d. Undefined

3. _____ is one of the most important functions in mathematics. A function commonly used to study growth and decay
   a. Exponential function0
   b. Thing
   c. Undefined
   d. Undefined

4. In mathematics, a _____ of a number x is the exponent y of the power by such that $x = b^y$. The value used for the base b must be neither 0 nor 1, nor a root of 1 in the case of the extension to complex numbers, and is typically 10, e, or 2.
   a. Logarithm0
   b. Thing
   c. Undefined
   d. Undefined

5. The mathematical concept of a _____ expresses the intuitive idea of deterministic dependence between two quantities, one of which is viewed as primary and the other as secondary. A _____ then is a way to associate a unique output for each input of a specified type, for example, a real number or an element of a given set.
   a. Function0
   b. Thing
   c. Undefined
   d. Undefined

6. The _____, the average in everyday English, which is also called the arithmetic _____ (and is distinguished from the geometric _____ or harmonic _____). The average is also called the sample _____. The expected value of a random variable, which is also called the population _____.
   a. Mean0
   b. Thing
   c. Undefined
   d. Undefined

7. A _____ is traditionally an infinitesimally small change in a variable.
   a. Differential0
   b. Thing
   c. Undefined
   d. Undefined

8. A _____ is a mathematical equation for an unknown function of one or several variables which relates the values of the function itself and of its derivatives of various orders.
   a. Thing
   b. Differential equation0
   c. Undefined
   d. Undefined

9. In mathematics, _____ occurs when the growth rate of a function is always proportional to the function's current size.
   a. Thing
   b. Exponential growth0
   c. Undefined
   d. Undefined

10. In mathematics and the mathematical sciences, a _____ is a fixed, but possibly unspecified, value. This is in contrast to a variable, which is not fixed.

Chapter 6. Applications of the Exponential and Natural Logarithm Functions

    a. Constant0
    c. Undefined
    b. Thing
    d. Undefined

11. In mathematics, two quantities are called _____ if they vary in such a way that one of the quantities is a constant multiple of the other, or equivalently if they have a constant ratio.
    a. Thing
    c. Undefined
    b. Proportional0
    d. Undefined

12. A _____ is a special kind of ratio, indicating a relationship between two measurements with different units, such as miles to gallons or cents to pounds.
    a. Thing
    c. Undefined
    b. Rate0
    d. Undefined

13. A _____ is a symbolic representation denoting a quantity or expression. It often represents an "unknown" quantity that has the potential to change.
    a. Thing
    c. Undefined
    b. Variable0
    d. Undefined

14. _____ is a special mathematical relationship between two quantities. Two quantities are called proportional if they vary in such a way that one of the quantities is a constant multiple of the other, or equivalently if they have a constant ratio.
    a. Proportionality0
    c. Undefined
    b. Thing
    d. Undefined

15. _____ is a synonym for information.
    a. Data0
    c. Undefined
    b. Thing
    d. Undefined

16. In sociology and biology a _____ is the collection of people or organisms of a particular species living in a given geographic area or space, usually measured by a census.
    a. Thing
    c. Undefined
    b. Population0
    d. Undefined

17. _____ is the process in which two clone daughter cells are produced by the cell division of one bacterium.
    a. Thing
    c. Undefined
    b. Bacteria growth0
    d. Undefined

18. Initial objects are also called _____, and terminal objects are also called final.
    a. Coterminal0
    c. Undefined
    b. Thing
    d. Undefined

19. _____ is a kind of property which exists as magnitude or multitude. It is among the basic classes of things along with quality, substance, change, and relation.
    a. Thing
    c. Undefined
    b. Amount0
    d. Undefined

Chapter 6. Applications of the Exponential and Natural Logarithm Functions

20. _____, or Drosophila Melanoaster is a two-winged insect that belongs to the Diptera, the order of the flies. The species is commonly known as the fruit fly, and is one of the most commonly used model organisms in biology, including studies in genetics, physiology and life history evolution.
    a. Thing
    b. Fruit flies0
    c. Undefined
    d. Undefined

21. An _____ or member of a set is an object that when collected together make up the set.
    a. Thing
    b. Element0
    c. Undefined
    d. Undefined

22. _____ is a decrease that follows an exponential function.
    a. Thing
    b. Exponential decay0
    c. Undefined
    d. Undefined

23. _____ is the property of a physical object that quantifies the amount of matter and energy it is equivalent to.
    a. Mass0
    b. Thing
    c. Undefined
    d. Undefined

24. In mathematics, in the field of group theory, a _____ of a group is a quasisimple subnormal subgroup.
    a. Concept
    b. Component0
    c. Undefined
    d. Undefined

25. _____ is the process in which an unstable atomic nucleus loses energy by emitting radiation in the form of particles or electromagnetic waves.
    a. Radioactive decay0
    b. Thing
    c. Undefined
    d. Undefined

26. _____ is a radiometric dating method that uses the naturally occurring isotope carbon-14 to determine the age of carbonaceous materials up to about 60,000 years.
    a. Radiocarbon dating0
    b. Thing
    c. Undefined
    d. Undefined

27. In geometry and physics, _____ are half-lines that continue forever in one direction.
    a. Rays0
    b. Thing
    c. Undefined
    d. Undefined

28. In economics, economic _____ is simply a state of the world where economic forces are balanced and in the absence of external influences the values of economic variables will not change.
    a. Thing
    b. Equilibrium0
    c. Undefined
    d. Undefined

29. A _____ is a quantity that denotes the proportional amount or magnitude of one quantity relative to another.
    a. Thing
    b. Ratio0
    c. Undefined
    d. Undefined

Chapter 6. Applications of the Exponential and Natural Logarithm Functions

30. _____ generally, is the synthesis of triose phospates and ultimately starch, glucose and other products from sunlight, carbon dioxide and water.
    - a. Thing
    - b. Photosynthesis0
    - c. Undefined
    - d. Undefined

31. In mathematics, a _____ is the result of multiplying, or an expression that identifies factors to be multiplied.
    - a. Product0
    - b. Thing
    - c. Undefined
    - d. Undefined

32. A _____ is an abstract model that uses mathematical language to describe the behavior of a system. Eykhoff defined a _____ as 'a representation of the essential aspects of an existing system which presents knowledge of that system in usable form'.
    - a. Mathematical model0
    - b. Thing
    - c. Undefined
    - d. Undefined

33. The _____ of a ring R is defined to be the smallest positive integer n such that $n\,a = 0$, for all a in R.
    - a. Thing
    - b. Characteristic0
    - c. Undefined
    - d. Undefined

34. In mathematics, factorization (British English: factorisation) or factoring is the decomposition of an object (for example, a number, a polynomial, or a matrix) into a product of other objects, or _____, which when multiplied together give the original.
    - a. Thing
    - b. Factors0
    - c. Undefined
    - d. Undefined

35. _____ is often used to describe the measurement of the steepness, incline, gradient, or grade of a straight line. The _____ is defined as the ratio of the "rise" divided by the "run" between two points on a line, or in other words, the ratio of the altitude change to the horizontal distance between any two points on the line.
    - a. Slope0
    - b. Thing
    - c. Undefined
    - d. Undefined

36. In trigonometry, the _____ is a function defined as $\tan x = \sin x / \cos x$. The function is so-named because it can be defined as the length of a certain segment of a _____ (in the geometric sense) to the unit circle. In plane geometry, a line is _____ to a curve, at some point, if both line and curve pass through the point with the same direction.
    - a. Thing
    - b. Tangent0
    - c. Undefined
    - d. Undefined

37. _____ has two distinct but etymologically-related meanings: one in geometry and one in trigonometry.
    - a. Tangent line0
    - b. Thing
    - c. Undefined
    - d. Undefined

38. In mathematics, the concept of a _____ tries to capture the intuitive idea of a geometrical one-dimensional and continuous object. A simple example is the circle.
    - a. Thing
    - b. Curve0
    - c. Undefined
    - d. Undefined

Chapter 6. Applications of the Exponential and Natural Logarithm Functions

39. In mathematics, a _____ is an n-tuple with n being 3.
    a. Thing
    b. Triple0
    c. Undefined
    d. Undefined

40. _____ is a subset of a population.
    a. Sample0
    b. Thing
    c. Undefined
    d. Undefined

41. The _____ of measurement are a globally standardized and modernized form of the metric system.
    a. Thing
    b. Units0
    c. Undefined
    d. Undefined

42. _____ are a measure of time.
    a. Minutes0
    b. Thing
    c. Undefined
    d. Undefined

43. In astronomy, geography, geometry and related sciences and contexts, a plane is said to be _____ at a given point if it is locally perpendicular to the gradient of the gravity field, i.e., with the direction of the gravitational force at that point.
    a. Horizontal0
    b. Thing
    c. Undefined
    d. Undefined

44. In mathematics, the _____ of two sets A and B is the set that contains all elements of A that also belong to B (or equivalently, all elements of B that also belong to A), but no other elements.
    a. Thing
    b. Intersection0
    c. Undefined
    d. Undefined

45. _____ is the fee paid on borrowed money.
    a. Interest0
    b. Thing
    c. Undefined
    d. Undefined

46. _____ interest refers to the fact that whenever interest is calculated, it is based not only on the original principal, but also on any unpaid interest that has been added to the principal.
    a. Compound0
    b. Thing
    c. Undefined
    d. Undefined

47. _____ refers to the fact that whenever interest is calculated, it is based not only on the original principal, but also on any unpaid interest that has been added to the principal. The more frequently interest is compounded, the faster the balance grows.
    a. Concept
    b. Compound interest0
    c. Undefined
    d. Undefined

48. In banking and accountancy, the outstanding _____ is the amount of money owned, or due, that remains in a deposit account or a loan account at a given date, after all past remittances, payments and withdrawal have been accounted for.

Chapter 6. Applications of the Exponential and Natural Logarithm Functions

a. Balance0
b. Thing
c. Undefined
d. Undefined

49. A _____ is 360° or 2δ radians.
   a. Thing
   b. Turn0
   c. Undefined
   d. Undefined

50. In business, particularly accounting, a _____ is the time intervals that the accounts, statement, payments, or other calculations cover.
   a. Thing
   b. Period0
   c. Undefined
   d. Undefined

51. In mathematics, a _____ is a statement that can be proved on the basis of explicitly stated or previously agreed assumptions.
   a. Thing
   b. Theorem0
   c. Undefined
   d. Undefined

52. A _____ is a deliberate process for transforming one or more inputs into one or more results.
   a. Calculation0
   b. Thing
   c. Undefined
   d. Undefined

53. A _____ function is a function for which, intuitively, small changes in the input result in small changes in the output.
   a. Event
   b. Continuous0
   c. Undefined
   d. Undefined

54. An _____ is the fee paid on borrow money.
   a. Concept
   b. Interest rate0
   c. Undefined
   d. Undefined

55. _____ or investing is a term with several closely-related meanings in business management, finance and economics, related to saving or deferring consumption.
   a. Thing
   b. Investment0
   c. Undefined
   d. Undefined

56. _____ of a single or multiple future payments is the nominal amounts of money to change hands at some future date, discounted to account for the time value of money, and other factors such as investment risk.
   a. Present value0
   b. Thing
   c. Undefined
   d. Undefined

57. In mathematics, the word _____ is used informally to refer to certain distinct bodies of knowledge about mathematics.
   a. Theoretical0
   b. Thing
   c. Undefined
   d. Undefined

Chapter 6. Applications of the Exponential and Natural Logarithm Functions

58. _____ is a mathematical subject that includes the study of limits, derivatives, integrals, and power series and constitutes a major part of modern university curriculum.
   a. Calculus0
   b. Thing
   c. Undefined
   d. Undefined

59. _____ is a term used in accounting, economics and finance with reference to the fact that assets with finite lives lose value over time.
   a. Thing
   b. Depreciation0
   c. Undefined
   d. Undefined

60. In mathematics, a _____ is the end result of a division problem. It can also be expressed as the number of times the divisor divides into the dividend.
   a. Quotient0
   b. Thing
   c. Undefined
   d. Undefined

61. The _____ is a measurement of how a function changes when the values of its inputs change.
   a. Derivative0
   b. Thing
   c. Undefined
   d. Undefined

62. The function difference divided by the point difference is known as the _____
   a. Difference quotient0
   b. Thing
   c. Undefined
   d. Undefined

63. A _____ are accounts maintained by commercial banks, savings and loan associations, credit unions, and mutual savings banks that pay interest but can not be used directly as money by, for example, writing a cheque.
   a. Savings account0
   b. Thing
   c. Undefined
   d. Undefined

64. _____ are the basic objects of study in graph theory. Informally speaking, a graph is a set of objects called points, nodes, or vertices connected by links called lines or edges.
   a. Thing
   b. Graphs0
   c. Undefined
   d. Undefined

65. A _____ is the result of the addition of a set of numbers. The numbers may be natural numbers, complex numbers, matrices, or still more complicated objects. An infinite _____ is a subtle procedure known as a series.
   a. Thing
   b. Sum0
   c. Undefined
   d. Undefined

66. _____ is a way of expressing a number as a fraction of 100 per cent meaning "per hundred".
   a. Thing
   b. Percent0
   c. Undefined
   d. Undefined

67. In economics, supply and _____ describe market relations between prospective sellers and buyers of a good.
   a. Demand0
   b. Thing
   c. Undefined
   d. Undefined

Chapter 6. Applications of the Exponential and Natural Logarithm Functions

68. In economics and business studies, the _____ is an elasticity that measures the nature and degree of the relationship between changes in quantity demanded of a good and changes in its price.
    a. Thing
    b. Elasticity of demand0
    c. Undefined
    d. Undefined

69. _____ is a business term for the amount of money that a company receives from its activities in a given period, mostly from sales of products and/or services to customers
    a. Thing
    b. Revenue0
    c. Undefined
    d. Undefined

70. In mathematics, the _____ is a conic section generated by the intersection of a right circular conical surface and a plane parallel to a generating straight line of that surface. It can also be defined as locus of points in a plane which are equidistant from a given point.
    a. Thing
    b. Parabola0
    c. Undefined
    d. Undefined

71. _____ is the middle point of a line segment.
    a. Midpoint0
    b. Thing
    c. Undefined
    d. Undefined

72. The _____ governs the differentiation of products of differentiable functions.
    a. Thing
    b. Product rule0
    c. Undefined
    d. Undefined

73. _____ is the ability to hold, receive or absorb, or a measure thereof, similar to the concept of volume.
    a. Concept
    b. Capacity0
    c. Undefined
    d. Undefined

74. In mathematics, an _____, mean, or central tendency of a data set refers to a measure of the "middle" or "expected" value of the data set.
    a. Average0
    b. Concept
    c. Undefined
    d. Undefined

75. _____ is the change in total cost that arises when the quantity produced changes by one unit.
    a. Marginal cost0
    b. Thing
    c. Undefined
    d. Undefined

76. In mathematics, the additive inverse, or _____ of a number n is the number that, when added to n, yields zero. The additive inverse of n is denoted −n. For example, 7 is −7, because 7 + (−7) = 0, and the additive inverse of −0.3 is 0.3, because −0.3 + 0.3 = 0.
    a. Thing
    b. Opposite0
    c. Undefined
    d. Undefined

77. In mathematics, the _____ of a number n is the number that, when added to n, yields zero. The _____ of n is denoted −n. For example, 7 is −7, because 7 + (−7) = 0, and the _____ of −0.3 is 0.3, because −0.3 + 0.3 = 0.

a. Additive inverse0
b. Thing
c. Undefined
d. Undefined

78. _____ of an object is its speed in a particular direction.
a. Thing
b. Velocity0
c. Undefined
d. Undefined

79. The _____ refers to a relationship between the duration of learning or experience and the resulting progress
a. Learning curve0
b. Thing
c. Undefined
d. Undefined

80. A central concept in science and the scientific method is that all evidence must be _____, or empirically based, that is, dependent on evidence or consequences that are observable by the senses.
a. Thing
b. Empirical0
c. Undefined
d. Undefined

81. _____ is the net action of matter particles or molecules, heat, momentum, or light whose end is to minimize a concentration gradient
a. Diffusion0
b. Thing
c. Undefined
d. Undefined

82. _____ Any process by which a specified characteristic usually amplitude of the output of a device is prevented from exceeding a predetermined value.
a. Limiting0
b. Thing
c. Undefined
d. Undefined

83. Deductive _____ is the kind of _____ in which the conclusion is necessitated by, or reached from, previously known facts (the premises).
a. Thing
b. Reasoning0
c. Undefined
d. Undefined

84. _____ is essentially exponential growth based on a constant rate of compound interest.
a. Exponential growth model0
b. Thing
c. Undefined
d. Undefined

85. One of the three formats applicable to a quadratic function is the _____ which is defined as $f = ax^2 + bx + c$.
a. Thing
b. General form0
c. Undefined
d. Undefined

86. A _____ models the S-curve of growth of some set P. The initial stage of growth is approximately exponential; then, as saturation begins, the growth slows, and at maturity, growth stops.
a. Thing
b. Logistic function0
c. Undefined
d. Undefined

87. In epidemiology, an _____ is a disease that appears as new cases in a given human population, during a given period, at a rate that substantially exceeds with is "expected," based on recent experience.

Chapter 6. Applications of the Exponential and Natural Logarithm Functions 71

  a. Thing
  c. Undefined
  b. Epidemic0
  d. Undefined

88. _____ is a a point on a curve at which the tangent crosses the curve itself.
  a. Inflection point0
  c. Undefined
  b. Thing
  d. Undefined

89. In geometry, the relations of _____ are those such as 'lies on' between points and lines (as in 'point P lies on line L'), and 'intersects' (as in 'line L_1 intersects line L_2', in three-dimensional space). That is, they are the binary relations describing how subsets meet.
  a. Thing
  c. Undefined
  b. Incidence0
  d. Undefined

90. _____ is the level of functional and/or metabolic efficiency of an organism at both the micro level.
  a. Health0
  c. Undefined
  b. Thing
  d. Undefined

91. In mathematics, _____ expressions is used to reduce the expression into the lowest possible term.
  a. Simplifying0
  c. Undefined
  b. Thing
  d. Undefined

92. In mathematics, there are several meanings of _____ depending on the subject.
  a. Thing
  c. Undefined
  b. Degree0
  d. Undefined

93. In geometry, the _____ of a vertex of a polyhedron is the amount by which the sum of the angles of the faces at the vertex falls short of a full circle.
  a. Thing
  c. Undefined
  b. Defect0
  d. Undefined

94. The _____ of a solid object is the three-dimensional concept of how much space it occupies, often quantified numerically.
  a. Volume0
  c. Undefined
  b. Thing
  d. Undefined

95. In calculus, the _____ is a formula for the derivative of the composite of two functions.
  a. Chain rule0
  c. Undefined
  b. Concept
  d. Undefined

96. In the scientific method, an _____ (Latin: ex-+-periri, "of (or from) trying"), is a set of actions and observations, performed in the context of solving a particular problem or question, in order to support or falsify a hypothesis or research concerning phenomena.
  a. Thing
  c. Undefined
  b. Experiment0
  d. Undefined

97. In physics, a _____ may refer to the scalar _____ or to the vector _____.

a. Potential0
c. Undefined
b. Thing
d. Undefined

98. _____ is a state located in the southern and southwestern regions of the United States of America.
a. Thing
c. Undefined
b. Texas0
d. Undefined

Chapter 7. The Definite Integral

1. A _____ is a quadrilateral, which is defined as a shape with four sides, which has a pair of parallel sides.
   a. Trapezoid0
   b. Thing
   c. Undefined
   d. Undefined

2. A _____ signifies a point or points of probability on a subject e.g., the _____ of creativity, which allows for the formation of rule or norm or law by interpretation of the phenomena events that can be created.
   a. Thing
   b. Principle0
   c. Undefined
   d. Undefined

3. _____ is often used to describe the measurement of the steepness, incline, gradient, or grade of a straight line. The _____ is defined as the ratio of the "rise" divided by the "run" between two points on a line, or in other words, the ratio of the altitude change to the horizontal distance between any two points on the line.
   a. Slope0
   b. Thing
   c. Undefined
   d. Undefined

4. In geometry, a line _____ is a part of a line that is bounded by two end points, and contains every point on the line between its end points.
   a. Concept
   b. Segment0
   c. Undefined
   d. Undefined

5. A _____ is a part of a line that is bounded by two end points, and contains every point on the line between its end points.
   a. Line segment0
   b. Thing
   c. Undefined
   d. Undefined

6. In mathematics, the concept of a _____ tries to capture the intuitive idea of a geometrical one-dimensional and continuous object. A simple example is the circle.
   a. Thing
   b. Curve0
   c. Undefined
   d. Undefined

7. In mathematics, _____ are the intuitive idea of a geometrical one-dimensional and continuous object.
   a. Thing
   b. Curves0
   c. Undefined
   d. Undefined

8. _____ is an extension of the concept of a sum.
   a. Thing
   b. Definite integral0
   c. Undefined
   d. Undefined

9. The _____ of a function is an extension of the concept of a sum, and are identified or found through the use of integration.
   a. Integral0
   b. Thing
   c. Undefined
   d. Undefined

10. _____ is a mathematical subject that includes the study of limits, derivatives, integrals, and power series and constitutes a major part of modern university curriculum.

a. Calculus0
b. Thing
c. Undefined
d. Undefined

11. _____ in calculus is primitive or indefinite integral of a function f is a function F whose derivative is equal to f, i.e., F Œ = f. The process of solving for antiderivatives is _____
   a. Thing
   b. Antidifferentiation0
   c. Undefined
   d. Undefined

12. The _____ is a measurement of how a function changes when the values of its inputs change.
   a. Derivative0
   b. Thing
   c. Undefined
   d. Undefined

13. _____, a field in mathematics, is the study of how functions change when their inputs change. The primary object of study in _____ is the derivative.
   a. Differential calculus0
   b. Thing
   c. Undefined
   d. Undefined

14. The mathematical concept of a _____ expresses the intuitive idea of deterministic dependence between two quantities, one of which is viewed as primary and the other as secondary. A _____ then is a way to associate a unique output for each input of a specified type, for example, a real number or an element of a given set.
   a. Thing
   b. Function0
   c. Undefined
   d. Undefined

15. A _____ is a special kind of ratio, indicating a relationship between two measurements with different units, such as miles to gallons or cents to pounds.
   a. Rate0
   b. Thing
   c. Undefined
   d. Undefined

16. In mathematics and the mathematical sciences, a _____ is a fixed, but possibly unspecified, value. This is in contrast to a variable, which is not fixed.
   a. Thing
   b. Constant0
   c. Undefined
   d. Undefined

17. _____ is a kind of property which exists as magnitude or multitude. It is among the basic classes of things along with quality, substance, change, and relation.
   a. Thing
   b. Amount0
   c. Undefined
   d. Undefined

18. An _____ of a function f is a function F whose derivative is equal to f, i.e., F' = f.
   a. Antiderivative0
   b. Thing
   c. Undefined
   d. Undefined

19. In mathematics, a _____ is a statement that can be proved on the basis of explicitly stated or previously agreed assumptions.

Chapter 7. The Definite Integral

    a. Theorem0
    b. Thing
    c. Undefined
    d. Undefined

20. In mathematics, the _____ f is the collection of all ordered pairs . In particular, graph means the graphical representation of this collection, in the form of a curve or surface, together with axes, etc. Graphing on a Cartesian plane is sometimes referred to as curve sketching.
    a. Graph of a function0
    b. Thing
    c. Undefined
    d. Undefined

21. In trigonometry, the _____ is a function defined as $\tan x = \sin x / \cos x$. The function is so-named because it can be defined as the length of a certain segment of a _____ (in the geometric sense) to the unit circle. In plane geometry, a line is _____ to a curve, at some point, if both line and curve pass through the point with the same direction.
    a. Tangent0
    b. Thing
    c. Undefined
    d. Undefined

22. In astronomy, geography, geometry and related sciences and contexts, a plane is said to be _____ at a given point if it is locally perpendicular to the gradient of the gravity field, i.e., with the direction of the gravitational force at that point.
    a. Thing
    b. Horizontal0
    c. Undefined
    d. Undefined

23. A _____ is a symbolic representation denoting a quantity or expression. It often represents an "unknown" quantity that has the potential to change.
    a. Variable0
    b. Thing
    c. Undefined
    d. Undefined

24. Mathematical _____ is used to represent ideas.
    a. Thing
    b. Notation0
    c. Undefined
    d. Undefined

25. _____ is the fee paid on borrowed money.
    a. Interest0
    b. Thing
    c. Undefined
    d. Undefined

26. In mathematics, defined and _____ are used to explain whether or not expressions have meaningful, sensible, and unambiguous values.
    a. Undefined0
    b. Thing
    c. Undefined
    d. Undefined

27. A _____ is the result of the addition of a set of numbers. The numbers may be natural numbers, complex numbers, matrices, or still more complicated objects. An infinite _____ is a subtle procedure known as a series.
    a. Thing
    b. Sum0
    c. Undefined
    d. Undefined

28. In calculus, the _____ in differentiation is a method of finding the derivative of a function that is the sum of two other functions for which derivatives exist.

a. Sum Rule0
b. Thing
c. Undefined
d. Undefined

29. A _____ of a number is the product of that number with any integer.
    a. Multiple0
    b. Thing
    c. Undefined
    d. Undefined

30. _____ of an object is its speed in a particular direction.
    a. Velocity0
    b. Thing
    c. Undefined
    d. Undefined

31. The metre (or _____, see spelling differences) is a measure of length. It is the basic unit of length in the metric system and in the International System of Units (SI), used around the world for general and scientific purposes.
    a. Meter0
    b. Concept
    c. Undefined
    d. Undefined

32. A _____ is a vehicle, missile or aircraft which obtains thrust by the reaction to the ejection of fast moving fluid from within a _____ engine.
    a. Thing
    b. Rocket0
    c. Undefined
    d. Undefined

33. The _____ of measurement are a globally standardized and modernized form of the metric system.
    a. Units0
    b. Thing
    c. Undefined
    d. Undefined

34. _____ is the change in total cost that arises when the quantity produced changes by one unit.
    a. Thing
    b. Marginal cost0
    c. Undefined
    d. Undefined

35. A _____ is a negotiable instrument instructing a financial institution to pay a specific amount of a specific currency from a specific demand account held in the maker/depositor's name with that institution. Both the maker and payee may be natural persons or legal entities.
    a. Check0
    b. Thing
    c. Undefined
    d. Undefined

36. A _____ is a set of numbers that designate location in a given reference system, such as x,y in a planar _____ system or an x,y,z in a three-dimensional _____ system.
    a. Thing
    b. Coordinate0
    c. Undefined
    d. Undefined

37. In mathematics and its applications, a _____ is a system for assigning an n-tuple of numbers or scalars to each point in an n-dimensional space.
    a. Coordinate system0
    b. Concept
    c. Undefined
    d. Undefined

38. Initial objects are also called _____, and terminal objects are also called final.

Chapter 7. The Definite Integral

    a. Coterminal0
    c. Undefined
    b. Thing
    d. Undefined

39. _____, Greek for "knowledge of nature," is the branch of science concerned with the discovery and characterization of universal laws which govern matter, energy, space, and time.
    a. Physics0
    c. Undefined
    b. Thing
    d. Undefined

40. _____ is, or relates to, the _____ temperature scale .
    a. Thing
    c. Undefined
    b. Celsius0
    d. Undefined

41. In mathematics, there are several meanings of _____ depending on the subject.
    a. Thing
    c. Undefined
    b. Degree0
    d. Undefined

42. _____ is a physical property of a system that underlies the common notions of hot and cold; something that is hotter has the greater _____.
    a. Thing
    c. Undefined
    b. Temperature0
    d. Undefined

43. In mathematics a _____ is a function which defines a distance between elements of a set.
    a. Metric0
    c. Undefined
    b. Thing
    d. Undefined

44. The _____ .
    a. Thing
    c. Undefined
    b. British thermal unit0
    d. Undefined

45. _____ are the basic objects of study in graph theory. Informally speaking, a graph is a set of objects called points, nodes, or vertices connected by links called lines or edges.
    a. Thing
    c. Undefined
    b. Graphs0
    d. Undefined

46. An _____ is a combination of numbers, operators, grouping symbols and/or free variables and bound variables arranged in a meaningful way which can be evaluated..
    a. Thing
    c. Undefined
    b. Expression0
    d. Undefined

47. In Euclidean geometry, an _____ is a closed segment of a differentiable curve in the two-dimensional plane; for example, a circular _____ is a segment of a circle.
    a. Concept
    c. Undefined
    b. Arc0
    d. Undefined

48. An _____ or an extremal point is a point that belongs to the extremity of something.

a. Thing
b. Extreme point0
c. Undefined
d. Undefined

49. One of the three formats applicable to a quadratic function is the _____ which is defined as f = ax² + bx + c.
a. General form0
b. Thing
c. Undefined
d. Undefined

50. A _____ function is a function for which, intuitively, small changes in the input result in small changes in the output.
a. Event
b. Continuous0
c. Undefined
d. Undefined

51. The _____ integers are all the integers from zero on upwards.
a. Nonnegative0
b. Thing
c. Undefined
d. Undefined

52. In elementary algebra, an _____ is a set that contains every real number between two indicated numbers and may contain the two numbers themselves.
a. Interval0
b. Thing
c. Undefined
d. Undefined

53. _____ is a method for approximating the values of integrals.
a. Riemann sum0
b. Thing
c. Undefined
d. Undefined

54. In geometry, a _____ is defined as a quadrilateral where all four of its angles are right angles.
a. Thing
b. Rectangle0
c. Undefined
d. Undefined

55. Generally, a _____ is a splitting of something into parts.
a. Partition0
b. Thing
c. Undefined
d. Undefined

56. _____ is the middle point of a line segment.
a. Midpoint0
b. Thing
c. Undefined
d. Undefined

57. The act of _____ is the calculated approximation of a result which is usable even if input data may be incomplete, uncertain, or noisy.
a. Thing
b. Estimating0
c. Undefined
d. Undefined

58. A _____ is an abstract model that uses mathematical language to describe the behavior of a system. Eykhoff defined a _____ as 'a representation of the essential aspects of an existing system which presents knowledge of that system in usable form'.

Chapter 7. The Definite Integral

a. Mathematical model0
c. Undefined
b. Thing
d. Undefined

59. In geometry, an _____ is a point at which a line segment or ray terminates.
   a. Thing
   b. Endpoint0
   c. Undefined
   d. Undefined

60. In mathematics, an inequality is a statement about the relative size or order of two objects. For example 14 > 10, or 14 is _____ 10.
   a. Thing
   b. Greater than0
   c. Undefined
   d. Undefined

61. _____ is a synonym for information.
   a. Thing
   b. Data0
   c. Undefined
   d. Undefined

62. _____ is the transport of people on a trip/journey or the process or time involved in a person or object moving from one location to another.
   a. Travel0
   b. Thing
   c. Undefined
   d. Undefined

63. In mathematics, a _____ is an ordered list of objects. Like a set, it contains members, also called elements or terms, and the number of terms is called the length of the _____. Unlike a set, order matters, and the exact same elements can appear multiple times at different positions in the _____.
   a. Sequence0
   b. Thing
   c. Undefined
   d. Undefined

64. A _____ is one of the basic shapes of geometry: a polygon with three vertices and three sides which are straight line segments.
   a. Triangle0
   b. Thing
   c. Undefined
   d. Undefined

65. In Euclidean geometry, a _____ is the set of all points in a plane at a fixed distance, called the radius, from a given point, the center.
   a. Thing
   b. Circle0
   c. Undefined
   d. Undefined

66. A _____ is a deliberate process for transforming one or more inputs into one or more results.
   a. Calculation0
   b. Thing
   c. Undefined
   d. Undefined

67. The _____ of a solid object is the three-dimensional concept of how much space it occupies, often quantified numerically.
   a. Thing
   b. Volume0
   c. Undefined
   d. Undefined

Chapter 7. The Definite Integral

68. In plane geometry, a _____ is a polygon with four equal sides, four right angles, and parallel opposite sides. In algebra, the _____ of a number is that number multiplied by itself.
 a. Square0
 b. Thing
 c. Undefined
 d. Undefined

69. _____ is the extra revenue that an additional unit of product will bring a firm. It can also be described as the change in total revenue/change in number of units sold.
 a. Thing
 b. Marginal revenue0
 c. Undefined
 d. Undefined

70. _____ is a business term for the amount of money that a company receives from its activities in a given period, mostly from sales of products and/or services to customers
 a. Revenue0
 b. Thing
 c. Undefined
 d. Undefined

71. In number theory, the _____ of arithmetic (or unique factorization theorem) states that every natural number greater than 1 can be written as a unique product of prime numbers.
 a. Fundamental theorem0
 b. Concept
 c. Undefined
 d. Undefined

72. _____ Any process by which a specified characteristic usually amplitude of the output of a device is prevented from exceeding a predetermined value.
 a. Limiting0
 b. Thing
 c. Undefined
 d. Undefined

73. The plus and _____ signs are mathematical symbols used to represent the notions of positive and negative as well as the operations of addition and subtraction.
 a. Thing
 b. Minus0
 c. Undefined
 d. Undefined

74. In topology and related areas of mathematics a _____ or Moore-Smith sequence is a generalization of a sequence, intended to unify the various notions of limit and generalize them to arbitrary topological spaces.
 a. Net0
 b. Thing
 c. Undefined
 d. Undefined

75. _____ or arithmetics is the oldest and most elementary branch of mathematics, used by almost everyone, for tasks ranging from simple daily counting to advanced science and business calculations.
 a. Arithmetic0
 b. Thing
 c. Undefined
 d. Undefined

76. _____, either of the curved-bracket punctuation marks that together make a set of _____
 a. Thing
 b. Parentheses0
 c. Undefined
 d. Undefined

77. A frame of _____ is a particular perspective from which the universe is observed.

Chapter 7. The Definite Integral

a. Thing
b. Reference0
c. Undefined
d. Undefined

78. In business, particularly accounting, a _____ is the time intervals that the accounts, statement, payments, or other calculations cover.
    a. Thing
    b. Period0
    c. Undefined
    d. Undefined

79. The deductive-nomological model is a formalized view of scientific _____ in natural language.
    a. Explanation0
    b. Thing
    c. Undefined
    d. Undefined

80. _____ of calculus is the statement that the two central operations of calculus, differentiation and integration, are inverse operations: if a continuous function is first integrated and then differentiated, the original function is retrieved.
    a. Fundamental Theorem of Calculus0
    b. Thing
    c. Undefined
    d. Undefined

81. In mathematics, science including computer science, linguistics and engineering, an _____ is, generally speaking, an independent variable or input to a function.
    a. Thing
    b. Argument0
    c. Undefined
    d. Undefined

82. In mathematics, a _____ is the end result of a division problem. It can also be expressed as the number of times the divisor divides into the dividend.
    a. Quotient0
    b. Thing
    c. Undefined
    d. Undefined

83. _____ has many meanings, most of which simply .
    a. Power0
    b. Thing
    c. Undefined
    d. Undefined

84. _____, from Latin meaning "to make progress", is defined in two different ways. Pure economic _____ is the increase in wealth that an investor has from making an investment, taking into consideration all costs associated with that investment including the opportunity cost of capital.
    a. Profit0
    b. Thing
    c. Undefined
    d. Undefined

85. In economics, supply and _____ describe market relations between prospective sellers and buyers of a good.
    a. Thing
    b. Demand0
    c. Undefined
    d. Undefined

86. Graphing on a Cartesian plane is sometimes referred to as _____.
    a. Thing
    b. Curve sketching0
    c. Undefined
    d. Undefined

Chapter 7. The Definite Integral

87. In mathematical analysis and related areas of mathematics, a set is called _____, if it is, in a certain sense, of finite size.
    a. Thing
    b. Bounded0
    c. Undefined
    d. Undefined

88. In mathematics, the _____ of two sets A and B is the set that contains all elements of A that also belong to B (or equivalently, all elements of B that also belong to A), but no other elements.
    a. Intersection0
    b. Thing
    c. Undefined
    d. Undefined

89. A _____ is a function for which, intuitively, small changes in the input result in small changes in the output.
    a. Event
    b. Continuous function0
    c. Undefined
    d. Undefined

90. In mathematics, an _____, mean, or central tendency of a data set refers to a measure of the "middle" or "expected" value of the data set.
    a. Concept
    b. Average0
    c. Undefined
    d. Undefined

91. The _____ is the total number of human beings alive on the planet Earth at a given time.
    a. World population0
    b. Thing
    c. Undefined
    d. Undefined

92. In sociology and biology a _____ is the collection of people or organisms of a particular species living in a given geographic area or space, usually measured by a census.
    a. Thing
    b. Population0
    c. Undefined
    d. Undefined

93. In mathematics, _____ growth occurs when the growth rate of a function is always proportional to the function's current size.
    a. Thing
    b. Exponential0
    c. Undefined
    d. Undefined

94. A _____ is an individual or household that purchases and uses goods and services generated within the economy.
    a. Consumer0
    b. Thing
    c. Undefined
    d. Undefined

95. _____ can be defined as the graph depicting the relationship between the price of a certain commodity, and the amount of it that consumers are willing and able to purchase at that given price demand.
    a. Thing
    b. Demand curve0
    c. Undefined
    d. Undefined

96. In mathematics, factorization (British English: factorisation) or factoring is the decomposition of an object (for example, a number, a polynomial, or a matrix) into a product of other objects, or _____, which when multiplied together give the original.

a. Thing
b. Factors0
c. Undefined
d. Undefined

97. In economics, _____ describe market relations between prospective sellers and buyers of a good.
a. Supply and demand0
b. Thing
c. Undefined
d. Undefined

98. _____ is a function that extends the concept of an ordinary sum
a. Thing
b. Integrand0
c. Undefined
d. Undefined

99. In banking and accountancy, the outstanding _____ is the amount of money owned, or due, that remains in a deposit account or a loan account at a given date, after all past remittances, payments and withdrawal have been accounted for.
a. Balance0
b. Thing
c. Undefined
d. Undefined

100. _____ is a regular and continuing flow of money generated by a business or investment
a. Income stream0
b. Thing
c. Undefined
d. Undefined

101. An _____ is the fee paid on borrow money.
a. Concept
b. Interest rate0
c. Undefined
d. Undefined

102. _____ measures the nominal future sum of money that a given sum of money is "worth" at a specified time in the future assuming a certain interest rate; this value does not include corrections for inflation or other factors that affect the true value of money in the future.
a. Future value0
b. Thing
c. Undefined
d. Undefined

103. In mathematics, _____ geometry was the traditional name for the geometry of three-dimensional Euclidean space — for practical purposes the kind of space we live in.
a. Solid0
b. Thing
c. Undefined
d. Undefined

104. In mathematics, a _____ is a quadric surface, with the following equation in Cartesian coordinates: $(x/a)^2 + (y/b)^2 = 1$.
a. Thing
b. Cylinder0
c. Undefined
d. Undefined

105. In classical geometry, a _____ of a circle or sphere is any line segment from its center to its boundary. By extension, the _____ of a circle or sphere is the length of any such segment. The _____ is half the diameter. In science and engineering the term _____ of curvature is commonly used as a synonym for _____.

Chapter 7. The Definite Integral

a. Radius0
b. Thing
c. Undefined
d. Undefined

106. _____ is a three-dimensional geometric shape formed by straight lines through a fixed point vertex to the points of a fixed curve directrix.
a. Thing
b. Right circular cone0
c. Undefined
d. Undefined

107. A _____ is a three-dimensional geometric shape formed by straight lines through a fixed point (vertex) to the points of a fixed curve (directrix)
a. Cone0
b. Concept
c. Undefined
d. Undefined

108. _____ or investing is a term with several closely-related meanings in business management, finance and economics, related to saving or deferring consumption.
a. Investment0
b. Thing
c. Undefined
d. Undefined

109. A _____ are accounts maintained by commercial banks, savings and loan associations, credit unions, and mutual savings banks that pay interest but can not be used directly as money by, for example, writing a cheque.
a. Thing
b. Savings account0
c. Undefined
d. Undefined

110. _____ of a single or multiple future payments is the nominal amounts of money to change hands at some future date, discounted to account for the time value of money, and other factors such as investment risk.
a. Present value0
b. Thing
c. Undefined
d. Undefined

111. _____ is a process of combining or accumulating. It may also refer to:
a. Integration0
b. Thing
c. Undefined
d. Undefined

112. _____ is a tool for finding antiderivatives and integrals. Using the fundamental theorem of calculus often requires finding an antiderivative. For this and other reasons, this rule is a relatively important tool for mathematicians. It is the counterpart to the chain rule of differentiation.
a. Thing
b. Integration by substitution0
c. Undefined
d. Undefined

113. In calculus, the _____ is a formula for the derivative of the composite of two functions.
a. Chain rule0
b. Concept
c. Undefined
d. Undefined

114. In mathematics, a _____ of a positive integer n is a way of writing n as a sum of positive integers.
a. Thing
b. Composition0
c. Undefined
d. Undefined

115. In mathematics, a _____, formed by the composition of one function on another, represents the application of the former to the result of the application of the latter to the argument of the composite.
   a. Thing
   b. Function composition0
   c. Undefined
   d. Undefined

116. In mathematics, a _____ is the result of multiplying, or an expression that identifies factors to be multiplied.
   a. Thing
   b. Product0
   c. Undefined
   d. Undefined

117. The _____ governs the differentiation of products of differentiable functions.
   a. Thing
   b. Product rule0
   c. Undefined
   d. Undefined

118. A _____ is a set of possible values that a variable can take on in order to satisfy a given set of conditions, which may include equations and inequalities.
   a. Solution set0
   b. Thing
   c. Undefined
   d. Undefined

119. _____ interest refers to the fact that whenever interest is calculated, it is based not only on the original principal, but also on any unpaid interest that has been added to the principal.
   a. Thing
   b. Compound0
   c. Undefined
   d. Undefined

120. _____ refers to the fact that whenever interest is calculated, it is based not only on the original principal, but also on any unpaid interest that has been added to the principal. The more frequently interest is compounded, the faster the balance grows.
   a. Concept
   b. Compound interest0
   c. Undefined
   d. Undefined

121. An _____ is the limit of a definite integral, as an endpoint of the interval of integration approaches either a specified real number or ‡ or − ‡ or, in some cases, as both endpoints approach limits.
   a. Thing
   b. Improper integral0
   c. Undefined
   d. Undefined

122. In mathematics, a _____ of a number x is the exponent y of the power by such that $x = b^y$. The value used for the base b must be neither 0 nor 1, nor a root of 1 in the case of the extension to complex numbers, and is typically 10, e, or 2.
   a. Logarithm0
   b. Thing
   c. Undefined
   d. Undefined

123. _____ is the state of being greater than any finite real or natural number, however large.
   a. Thing
   b. Infinite0
   c. Undefined
   d. Undefined

124. In mathematics, _____ describes an entity with a limit.

a. Thing
c. Undefined
b. Convergent0
d. Undefined

125. In mathematics, a _____ series is an infinite series that is not convergent, meaning that the infinite sequence of the partial sums of the series does not have a limit.
   a. Thing
   c. Undefined
   b. Divergent0
   d. Undefined

126. A _____ is a one-dimensional picture in which the integers are shown as specially-marked points evenly spaced on a line.
   a. Number line0
   c. Undefined
   b. Thing
   d. Undefined

127. _____ is the chance that something is likely to happen or be the case.
   a. Probability0
   c. Undefined
   b. Thing
   d. Undefined

128. In mathematics, a set is called _____ if there is a bijection between the set and some set of the form {1, 2, ..., n} where n is a natural number.
   a. Thing
   c. Undefined
   b. Finite0
   d. Undefined

129. _____ are economic entities that give rise to future economic benefit and is controlled by the entity as a result of past transaction or other events
   a. Asset0
   c. Undefined
   b. Thing
   d. Undefined

130. A _____ is 360° or 2δ radians.
   a. Thing
   c. Undefined
   b. Turn0
   d. Undefined

131. _____ is a special mathematical relationship between two quantities.Two quantities are called proportional if they vary in such a way that one of the quantities is a constant multiple of the other, or equivalently if they have a constant ratio.
   a. Proportionality0
   c. Undefined
   b. Thing
   d. Undefined

132. In mathematical analysis, _____ are objects which generalize functions and probability distributions.
   a. Distribution0
   c. Undefined
   b. Thing
   d. Undefined

133. A _____ is a function that assigns a number to subsets of a given set.
   a. Thing
   c. Undefined
   b. Measure0
   d. Undefined

Chapter 7. The Definite Integral

134. The _____, the average in everyday English, which is also called the arithmetic _____ (and is distinguished from the geometric _____ or harmonic _____). The average is also called the sample _____. The expected value of a random variable, which is also called the population _____.
   a. Thing
   b. Mean0
   c. Undefined
   d. Undefined

135. _____ is a function that represents a probability distribution in terms of integrals.
   a. Thing
   b. Probability density function0
   c. Undefined
   d. Undefined

136. _____ is one of the most important functions in mathematics. A function commonly used to study growth and decay
   a. Thing
   b. Exponential function0
   c. Undefined
   d. Undefined

137. _____ is mass m per unit volume V.
   a. Thing
   b. Density0
   c. Undefined
   d. Undefined

138. If the probabilities of simple events are all the same, then they are _____. This occurs in a uniform sample space.
   a. Equally likely0
   b. Thing
   c. Undefined
   d. Undefined

139. In the scientific method, an _____ (Latin: ex-+-periri, "of (or from) trying"), is a set of actions and observations, performed in the context of solving a particular problem or question, in order to support or falsify a hypothesis or research concerning phenomena.
   a. Experiment0
   b. Thing
   c. Undefined
   d. Undefined

140. _____ are a measure of time.
   a. Minutes0
   b. Thing
   c. Undefined
   d. Undefined

141. In common philosophical language, a proposition or _____, is the content of an assertion, that is, it is true-or-false and defined by the meaning of a particular piece of language.
   a. Concept
   b. Statement0
   c. Undefined
   d. Undefined

142. _____ is electromagnetic radiation with a wavelength that is visible to the eye (visible _____) or, in a technical or scientific context, electromagnetic radiation of any wavelength.
   a. Light0
   b. Thing
   c. Undefined
   d. Undefined

143. The _____ rule, also known as a slipstick, is a mechanical analog computer, consisting of at least two finely divided scales, most often a fixed outer pair and a movable inner one, with a sliding window called the cursor.

a. Slide0
b. Thing
c. Undefined
d. Undefined

144. A _____ is a unit of length, usually used to measure distance, in a number of different systems, including Imperial units, United States customary units and Norwegian/Swedish mil. Its size can vary from system to system, but in each is between 1 and 10 kilometers. In contemporary English contexts _____ refers to either:
a. Thing
b. Mile0
c. Undefined
d. Undefined

145. A pair of angles is _____ if their respective measures sum to 180 degrees.
a. Concept
b. Supplementary0
c. Undefined
d. Undefined

146. Fixed costs are expenses whose total does not change in proportion to the activity of a business.Unit fixed costs decline with volume following a retangular hyperbola as the volume of production.Variable costs by contrast change in relation to the activity of a business such as sales or production volume.Along with variable costs,fixed costs make up one of the two components of total cost. In the most simple production function total cost is equal to fixed costs plus variable costs.In accounting terminology, fixed costs will broadly include all costs which are not included in cost of goods sold, and variable costs are those captured in costs of goods sold. The implicit assumption required to make the equivalence between the accounting and economics terminology is that the accounting period is equal to the period in which fixed costs do not vary in relation to production. In practice, this equivalence does not always hold and depending on the period under consideration by management, some overhead expenses can be adjusted by management, and the specific allocation of each expense to each category will be decided under cost accounting.In business planning and management accounting, usage of the terms fixed costs, variable costs and others will often differ from usage in economics, and may depend on the intended use. For example, costs may be segregated into per unit costs fixed costs per period, and variable costs as a proportion of revenue. Capital expenditures will usually be allocated separately, and depending on the purpose, a portion may be regularly allocated to expenses as depreciation and amortization and seen as a _____ per period, or the entire amount may be considered upfront fixed costs.
a. Thing
b. Fixed cost0
c. Undefined
d. Undefined

147. _____ are expenses whose total does not change in proportion to the activity of a business, within the relevant time period or scale of production
a. Thing
b. Fixed costs0
c. Undefined
d. Undefined

148. _____ is a list of goods and materials, or those goods and materials themselves, held available in stock by a business
a. Thing
b. Inventory0
c. Undefined
d. Undefined

149. A _____ is a unit of length in the metric system, equal to one thousand metres, the current SI base unit of length
a. Thing
b. Kilometer0
c. Undefined
d. Undefined

Chapter 8. Functions of Several Variables

1. A _____ is a symbolic representation denoting a quantity or expression. It often represents an "unknown" quantity that has the potential to change.
   a. Variable0
   b. Thing
   c. Undefined
   d. Undefined

2. _____ is a mathematical subject that includes the study of limits, derivatives, integrals, and power series and constitutes a major part of modern university curriculum.
   a. Thing
   b. Calculus0
   c. Undefined
   d. Undefined

3. The mathematical concept of a _____ expresses the intuitive idea of deterministic dependence between two quantities, one of which is viewed as primary and the other as secondary. A _____ then is a way to associate a unique output for each input of a specified type, for example, a real number or an element of a given set.
   a. Thing
   b. Function0
   c. Undefined
   d. Undefined

4. _____ is the fee paid on borrowed money.
   a. Thing
   b. Interest0
   c. Undefined
   d. Undefined

5. In mathematics, a _____ is the result of multiplying, or an expression that identifies factors to be multiplied.
   a. Product0
   b. Thing
   c. Undefined
   d. Undefined

6. _____ is the application of tools and a processing medium to the transformation of raw materials into finished goods for sale.
   a. Manufacturing0
   b. Thing
   c. Undefined
   d. Undefined

7. In computer science, an _____ is the problem of finding the best solution from all feasible solutions.
   a. Thing
   b. Optimization problem0
   c. Undefined
   d. Undefined

8. _____ is a process of combining or accumulating. It may also refer to:
   a. Integration0
   b. Thing
   c. Undefined
   d. Undefined

9. The _____ is a measurement of how a function changes when the values of its inputs change.
   a. Derivative0
   b. Thing
   c. Undefined
   d. Undefined

10. _____ is a business term for the amount of money that a company receives from its activities in a given period, mostly from sales of products and/or services to customers
    a. Revenue0
    b. Thing
    c. Undefined
    d. Undefined

Chapter 8. Functions of Several Variables

11. A _____ is a set of numbers that designate location in a given reference system, such as x,y in a planar _____ system or an x,y,z in a three-dimensional _____ system.
    a. Thing
    b. Coordinate0
    c. Undefined
    d. Undefined

12. In mathematics and its applications, a _____ is a system for assigning an n-tuple of numbers or scalars to each point in an n-dimensional space.
    a. Concept
    b. Coordinate system0
    c. Undefined
    d. Undefined

13. _____ is a set, with some particular properties and usually some additional structure, such as the operations of addition or multiplication, for instance.
    a. Space0
    b. Thing
    c. Undefined
    d. Undefined

14. _____ are the basic objects of study in graph theory. Informally speaking, a graph is a set of objects called points, nodes, or vertices connected by links called lines or edges.
    a. Graphs0
    b. Thing
    c. Undefined
    d. Undefined

15. In mathematics, factorization (British English: factorisation) or factoring is the decomposition of an object (for example, a number, a polynomial, or a matrix) into a product of other objects, or _____, which when multiplied together give the original.
    a. Thing
    b. Factors0
    c. Undefined
    d. Undefined

16. Compass and straightedge or ruler-and-compass _____ is the _____ of lengths or angles using only an idealized ruler and compass.
    a. Thing
    b. Construction0
    c. Undefined
    d. Undefined

17. In plane geometry, a _____ is a polygon with four equal sides, four right angles, and parallel opposite sides. In algebra, the _____ of a number is that number multiplied by itself.
    a. Square0
    b. Thing
    c. Undefined
    d. Undefined

18. The _____ of measurement are a globally standardized and modernized form of the metric system.
    a. Thing
    b. Units0
    c. Undefined
    d. Undefined

19. _____ is a kind of property which exists as magnitude or multitude. It is among the basic classes of things along with quality, substance, change, and relation.
    a. Amount0
    b. Thing
    c. Undefined
    d. Undefined

Chapter 8. Functions of Several Variables 91

20. A _____ is the result of the addition of a set of numbers. The numbers may be natural numbers, complex numbers, matrices, or still more complicated objects. An infinite _____ is a subtle procedure known as a series.
 a. Thing
 b. Sum0
 c. Undefined
 d. Undefined

21. The _____ of a solid object is the three-dimensional concept of how much space it occupies, often quantified numerically.
 a. Volume0
 b. Thing
 c. Undefined
 d. Undefined

22. _____ asserts that the maximum output of a technologically-determined production process is a mathematical function of input factors of production.
 a. Production function0
 b. Thing
 c. Undefined
 d. Undefined

23. The _____, the average in everyday English, which is also called the arithmetic _____ (and is distinguished from the geometric _____ or harmonic _____). The average is also called the sample _____. The expected value of a random variable, which is also called the population _____.
 a. Thing
 b. Mean0
 c. Undefined
 d. Undefined

24. In mathematics and the mathematical sciences, a _____ is a fixed, but possibly unspecified, value. This is in contrast to a variable, which is not fixed.
 a. Constant0
 b. Thing
 c. Undefined
 d. Undefined

25. In mathematics, the concept of a _____ tries to capture the intuitive idea of a geometrical one-dimensional and continuous object. A simple example is the circle.
 a. Curve0
 b. Thing
 c. Undefined
 d. Undefined

26. In mathematics, _____ are the intuitive idea of a geometrical one-dimensional and continuous object.
 a. Curves0
 b. Thing
 c. Undefined
 d. Undefined

27. In geometry, an _____ of a triangle is a straight line through a vertex and perpendicular to (i.e. forming a right angle with) the opposite side or an extension of the opposite side.
 a. Concept
 b. Altitude0
 c. Undefined
 d. Undefined

28. In combinatorial mathematics, a _____ is an un-ordered collection of unique elements.
 a. Concept
 b. Combination0
 c. Undefined
 d. Undefined

29. In topology and related areas of mathematics a _____ or Moore-Smith sequence is a generalization of a sequence, intended to unify the various notions of limit and generalize them to arbitrary topological spaces.

Chapter 8. Functions of Several Variables

    a. Net0
    b. Thing
    c. Undefined
    d. Undefined

30. A _____ is a special kind of ratio, indicating a relationship between two measurements with different units, such as miles to gallons or cents to pounds.
    a. Thing
    b. Rate0
    c. Undefined
    d. Undefined

31. An _____ is a rule or law which excepts certain things from another rule or law.
    a. Thing
    b. Exemption0
    c. Undefined
    d. Undefined

32. A _____ is a function that assigns a number to subsets of a given set.
    a. Measure0
    b. Thing
    c. Undefined
    d. Undefined

33. _____ of a function of several variables is its derivative with respect to one of those variables with the others held constant as opposed to the total derivative, in which all variables are allowed to vary.
    a. Thing
    b. Partial derivative0
    c. Undefined
    d. Undefined

34. In mathematics, a _____ is an expression that is constructed from one or more variables and constants, using only the operations of addition, subtraction, multiplication, and constant positive whole number exponents. is a _____. Note in particular that division by an expression containing a variable is not in general allowed in polynomials. [1]
    a. Thing
    b. Polynomial0
    c. Undefined
    d. Undefined

35. _____ has many meanings, most of which simply .
    a. Power0
    b. Thing
    c. Undefined
    d. Undefined

36. _____ is a method for differentiating expressions involving exponentiation the power operation.
    a. Thing
    b. Power rule0
    c. Undefined
    d. Undefined

37. _____ is often used to describe the measurement of the steepness, incline, gradient, or grade of a straight line. The _____ is defined as the ratio of the "rise" divided by the "run" between two points on a line, or in other words, the ratio of the altitude change to the horizontal distance between any two points on the line.
    a. Slope0
    b. Thing
    c. Undefined
    d. Undefined

38. In trigonometry, the _____ is a function defined as $\tan x = \sin x / \cos x$. The function is so-named because it can be defined as the length of a certain segment of a _____ (in the geometric sense) to the unit circle. In plane geometry, a line is _____ to a curve, at some point, if both line and curve pass through the point with the same direction.

Chapter 8. Functions of Several Variables

    a. Thing
    b. Tangent0
    c. Undefined
    d. Undefined

39. _____ has two distinct but etymologically-related meanings: one in geometry and one in trigonometry.
    a. Tangent line0
    b. Thing
    c. Undefined
    d. Undefined

40. In mathematics, a _____ is a two-dimensional manifold or surface that is perfectly flat.
    a. Plane0
    b. Thing
    c. Undefined
    d. Undefined

41. Transport or _____ is the movement of people and goods from one place to another.
    a. Thing
    b. Transportation0
    c. Undefined
    d. Undefined

42. In economics, supply and _____ describe market relations between prospective sellers and buyers of a good.
    a. Thing
    b. Demand0
    c. Undefined
    d. Undefined

43. In statistics, _____ means the most frequent value assumed by a random variable, or occurring in a sampling of a random variable.
    a. Concept
    b. Mode0
    c. Undefined
    d. Undefined

44. In mathematics, an _____, mean, or central tendency of a data set refers to a measure of the "middle" or "expected" value of the data set.
    a. Average0
    b. Concept
    c. Undefined
    d. Undefined

45. A _____ is an individual or household that purchases and uses goods and services generated within the economy.
    a. Thing
    b. Consumer0
    c. Undefined
    d. Undefined

46. In mathematics and logic, a _____ proof is a way of showing the truth or falsehood of a given statement by a straightforward combination of established facts, usually existing lemmas and theorems, without making any further assumptions.
    a. Thing
    b. Direct0
    c. Undefined
    d. Undefined

47. A _____ is a compensation which workers receive in exchange for their labor.
    a. Wage0
    b. Thing
    c. Undefined
    d. Undefined

48. The _____ or kilogramme is the SI base unit of mass. It is defined as being equal to the mass of the international prototype of the _____.

a. Kilogram0
b. Thing
c. Undefined
d. Undefined

49. The metre (or _____, see spelling differences) is a measure of length. It is the basic unit of length in the metric system and in the International System of Units (SI), used around the world for general and scientific purposes.
   a. Meter0
   b. Concept
   c. Undefined
   d. Undefined

50. _____ is a free computer algebra system based on a 1982 version of Macsyma
   a. Thing
   b. Maxima0
   c. Undefined
   d. Undefined

51. _____ are points in the domain of a function at which the function takes a largest value or smallest value, either within a given neighborhood or on the function domain in its entirety.
   a. Maxima and minima0
   b. Thing
   c. Undefined
   d. Undefined

52. An _____ is the fee paid on borrow money.
   a. Concept
   b. Interest rate0
   c. Undefined
   d. Undefined

53. In mathematics, maxima and _____, known collectively as extrema, are points in the domain of a function at which the function takes a largest value .
   a. Thing
   b. Minima0
   c. Undefined
   d. Undefined

54. The _____ is the highest point in a certain portion of a graph.
   a. Relative maximum0
   b. Thing
   c. Undefined
   d. Undefined

55. The _____ is the lowest point in a certain portion of a graph.
   a. Relative minimum0
   b. Thing
   c. Undefined
   d. Undefined

56. In astronomy, geography, geometry and related sciences and contexts, a plane is said to be _____ at a given point if it is locally perpendicular to the gradient of the gravity field, i.e., with the direction of the gravitational force at that point.
   a. Thing
   b. Horizontal0
   c. Undefined
   d. Undefined

57. Acid _____ ratio measures the ability of a company to use its near cash or quick assets to immediately extinguish its current liabilities.
   a. Test0
   b. Thing
   c. Undefined
   d. Undefined

58. _____ traditionally refers to the statistical process of determining comparable scores on different forms of an exam

Chapter 8. Functions of Several Variables

    a. Equating0
    c. Undefined
    b. Thing
    d. Undefined

59. An _____ is a combination of numbers, operators, grouping symbols and/or free variables and bound variables arranged in a meaningful way which can be evaluated..
    a. Thing
    c. Undefined
    b. Expression0
    d. Undefined

60. _____, from Latin meaning "to make progress", is defined in two different ways. Pure economic _____ is the increase in wealth that an investor has from making an investment, taking into consideration all costs associated with that investment including the opportunity cost of capital.
    a. Thing
    c. Undefined
    b. Profit0
    d. Undefined

61. In mathematics, a _____ is a condition that a solution to an optimization problem must satisfy in order to be acceptable.
    a. Constraint0
    c. Undefined
    b. Thing
    d. Undefined

62. In physics, a _____ may refer to the scalar _____ or to the vector _____.
    a. Thing
    c. Undefined
    b. Potential0
    d. Undefined

63. _____ determines whether a given stationary point of a function is a maximum or a minimum.
    a. Second derivative test0
    c. Undefined
    b. Thing
    d. Undefined

64. In a mathematical proof or a syllogism, a _____ is a statement that is the logical consequence of preceding statements.
    a. Conclusion0
    c. Undefined
    b. Concept
    d. Undefined

65. An _____ or an extremal point is a point that belongs to the extremity of something.
    a. Thing
    c. Undefined
    b. Extreme point0
    d. Undefined

66. _____ are a method for finding the extrema of a function of several variables subject to one or more constraints: it is the basic tool in nonlinear constrained optimization.
    a. Thing
    c. Undefined
    b. Lagrange multipliers0
    d. Undefined

67. A _____ is a three-dimensional geometric shape formed by straight lines through a fixed point (vertex) to the points of a fixed curve (directrix)
    a. Concept
    c. Undefined
    b. Cone0
    d. Undefined

Chapter 8. Functions of Several Variables

68. The term _____ refers to the largest and the smallest element of a set.
    a. Thing
    b. Extreme value0
    c. Undefined
    d. Undefined

69. A _____ is a quantity that denotes the proportional amount or magnitude of one quantity relative to another.
    a. Ratio0
    b. Thing
    c. Undefined
    d. Undefined

70. _____ is a circle with a unit radius, i.e., a circle whose radius is 1.
    a. Unit circle0
    b. Thing
    c. Undefined
    d. Undefined

71. In Euclidean geometry, a _____ is the set of all points in a plane at a fixed distance, called the radius, from a given point, the center.
    a. Thing
    b. Circle0
    c. Undefined
    d. Undefined

72. In geometry, a _____ is defined as a quadrilateral where all four of its angles are right angles.
    a. Rectangle0
    b. Thing
    c. Undefined
    d. Undefined

73. In mathematics, the _____ is a conic section generated by the intersection of a right circular conical surface and a plane parallel to a generating straight line of that surface. It can also be defined as locus of points in a plane which are equidistant from a given point.
    a. Parabola0
    b. Thing
    c. Undefined
    d. Undefined

74. In mathematics, _____ is an elementary arithmetic operation. When one of the numbers is a whole number, _____ is the repeated sum of the other number.
    a. Multiplication0
    b. Thing
    c. Undefined
    d. Undefined

75. In regression analysis, _____, also known as ordinary _____ analysis is a method for linear regression that determines the values of unknown quantities in a statistical model by minimizing the sum of the residuals difference between the predicted and observed values squared.
    a. Thing
    b. Least squares0
    c. Undefined
    d. Undefined

76. In geometry, the relations of _____ are those such as 'lies on' between points and lines (as in 'point P lies on line L'), and 'intersects' (as in 'line L_1 intersects line L_2', in three-dimensional space). That is, they are the binary relations describing how subsets meet.
    a. Incidence0
    b. Thing
    c. Undefined
    d. Undefined

77. _____ is a physical property of a system that underlies the common notions of hot and cold; something that is hotter has the greater _____.

Chapter 8. Functions of Several Variables

a. Thing
c. Undefined
b. Temperature0
d. Undefined

78. _____ is a synonym for information.
a. Data0
c. Undefined
b. Thing
d. Undefined

79. A _____ is a statement or claimt that a particular event will occur in the future in more certain terms than a forecast.
a. Thing
c. Undefined
b. Prediction0
d. Undefined

80. A _____ consists either of a suggested explanation for a phenomenon or of a reasoned proposal suggesting a possible correlation between multiple phenomena.
a. Thing
c. Undefined
b. Hypothesis0
d. Undefined

81. The word _____ comes from the Latin word linearis, which means created by lines.
a. Thing
c. Undefined
b. Linear0
d. Undefined

82. In common philosophical language, a proposition or _____, is the content of an assertion, that is, it is true-or-false and defined by the meaning of a particular piece of language.
a. Statement0
c. Undefined
b. Concept
d. Undefined

83. _____ is the level of functional and/or metabolic efficiency of an organism at both the micro level.
a. Health0
c. Undefined
b. Thing
d. Undefined

84. In mathematics, a _____ is a constant multiplicative factor of a certain object. The object can be such things as a variable, a vector, a function, etc. For example, the _____ of $9x^2$ is 9.
a. Coefficient0
c. Undefined
b. Thing
d. Undefined

85. U.S. liquid _____ is legally defined as 231 cubic inches, and is equal to 3.785411784 litres or abotu 0.13368 cubic feet. This is the most common definition of a _____. The U.S. fluid ounce is defined as 1/128 of a U.S. _____.
a. Gallon0
c. Undefined
b. Thing
d. Undefined

86. A _____ is a unit of length, usually used to measure distance, in a number of different systems, including Imperial units, United States customary units and Norwegian/Swedish mil. Its size can vary from system to system, but in each is between 1 and 10 kilometers. In contemporary English contexts _____ refers to either:

Chapter 8. Functions of Several Variables

a. Mile0
b. Thing
c. Undefined
d. Undefined

87. _____ is a way of expressing a number as a fraction of 100 per cent meaning "per hundred".
   a. Thing
   b. Percent0
   c. Undefined
   d. Undefined

88. In mathematics, the _____ of a function is the set of all "output" values produced by that function. Given a function $f: A \rightarrow B$, the _____ of f, is defined to be the set $\{x \in B : x = f(a) \text{ for some } a \in A\}$.
   a. Range0
   b. Thing
   c. Undefined
   d. Undefined

89. A _____ is a first degree polynomial mathematical function of the form: $f(x) = mx + b$ where m and b are real constants and x is a real variable.
   a. Thing
   b. Linear function0
   c. Undefined
   d. Undefined

90. _____, either of the curved-bracket punctuation marks that together make a set of _____
   a. Parentheses0
   b. Thing
   c. Undefined
   d. Undefined

91. _____ is a concept that permeates much of inferential statistics and descriptive statistics. More properly, it is "the sum of the squared deviations".
   a. Thing
   b. Sum of squares0
   c. Undefined
   d. Undefined

92. _____ systems represent systems whose behavior is not expressible as a sum of the behaviors of its descriptors.
   a. Thing
   b. Nonlinear0
   c. Undefined
   d. Undefined

93. A _____ is the quantity that defines certain relatively constant characteristics of systems or functions..
   a. Parameter0
   b. Thing
   c. Undefined
   d. Undefined

94. _____ is a regression method that models the relationship between a dependent variable Y, independent variables Xp, and a random term å.
   a. Linear regression0
   b. Thing
   c. Undefined
   d. Undefined

95. The _____ of a ring R is defined to be the smallest positive integer n such that $n\,a = 0$, for all a in R.
   a. Thing
   b. Characteristic0
   c. Undefined
   d. Undefined

96. A _____ is a unit of length in the metric system, equal to one thousand metres, the current SI base unit of length

Chapter 8. Functions of Several Variables 99

    a. Kilometer0   b. Thing
    c. Undefined   d. Undefined

97. _____, a field in mathematics, is the study of how functions change when their inputs change. The primary object of study in _____ is the derivative.
    a. Thing   b. Differential calculus0
    c. Undefined   d. Undefined

98. In mathematical analysis, _____ are objects which generalize functions and probability distributions.
    a. Thing   b. Distribution0
    c. Undefined   d. Undefined

99. A _____ of a number is the product of that number with any integer.
    a. Multiple0   b. Thing
    c. Undefined   d. Undefined

100. In mathematics, an _____ is any of the arguments, i.e. "inputs", to a function. Thus if we have a function f(x), then x is a _____.
    a. Thing   b. Independent variable0
    c. Undefined   d. Undefined

101. In mathematics, a matrix can be thought of as each row or _____ being a vector. Hence, a space formed by row vectors or _____ vectors are said to be a row space or a _____ space.
    a. Concept   b. Column0
    c. Undefined   d. Undefined

102. A _____ is a negotiable instrument instructing a financial institution to pay a specific amount of a specific currency from a specific demand account held in the maker/depositor's name with that institution. Both the maker and payee may be natural persons or legal entities.
    a. Thing   b. Check0
    c. Undefined   d. Undefined

103. _____ is the act of transforming data with the aim of extracting useful information and facilitating conclusions.
    a. Concept   b. Data analysis0
    c. Undefined   d. Undefined

104. Any point where a graph makes contact with an coordinate axis is called an _____ of the graph
    a. Thing   b. Intercept0
    c. Undefined   d. Undefined

105. In mathematics, there are several meanings of _____ depending on the subject.
    a. Degree0   b. Thing
    c. Undefined   d. Undefined

106. In mathematics and elsewhere, the adjective _____ means fourth order, such as the function x4. A _____ number is a number which equals the fourth power of an integer.

a. Quartic0
b. Thing
c. Undefined
d. Undefined

107. A _____ is a polynomial function of the form f(x) = ax² + bx +c , where a, b, c are real numbers and a , 0.
a. Event
b. Quadratic function0
c. Undefined
d. Undefined

108. In mathematics, _____ growth occurs when the growth rate of a function is always proportional to the function's current size.
a. Thing
b. Exponential0
c. Undefined
d. Undefined

109. A real-valued function f defined on the real line is said to have a _____ point at the point x∗, if there exists some ε > 0, such that f when x − x∗ < ε.
a. Local maximum0
b. Thing
c. Undefined
d. Undefined

110. _____ is a a point on a curve at which the tangent crosses the curve itself.
a. Inflection point0
b. Thing
c. Undefined
d. Undefined

111. The _____ integers are all the integers from zero on upwards.
a. Thing
b. Nonnegative0
c. Undefined
d. Undefined

112. The _____ of a function is an extension of the concept of a sum, and are identified or found through the use of integration.
a. Integral0
b. Thing
c. Undefined
d. Undefined

113. In elementary algebra, an _____ is a set that contains every real number between two indicated numbers and may contain the two numbers themselves.
a. Interval0
b. Thing
c. Undefined
d. Undefined

114. In mathematical analysis and related areas of mathematics, a set is called _____, if it is, in a certain sense, of finite size.
a. Thing
b. Bounded0
c. Undefined
d. Undefined

115. In mathematics, _____ geometry was the traditional name for the geometry of three-dimensional Euclidean space — for practical purposes the kind of space we live in.
a. Thing
b. Solid0
c. Undefined
d. Undefined

116. The plus and _____ signs are mathematical symbols used to represent the notions of positive and negative as well as the operations of addition and subtraction.
   a. Minus0
   b. Thing
   c. Undefined
   d. Undefined

117. _____ are objects, characters, or other concrete representations of ideas, concepts, or other abstractions.
   a. Symbols0
   b. Thing
   c. Undefined
   d. Undefined

118. An _____ of a function f is a function F whose derivative is equal to f, i.e., F' = f.
   a. Antiderivative0
   b. Thing
   c. Undefined
   d. Undefined

119. _____ is a function whose values do not vary and thus are constant.
   a. Thing
   b. Constant function0
   c. Undefined
   d. Undefined

120. A _____ function is a function for which, intuitively, small changes in the input result in small changes in the output.
   a. Event
   b. Continuous0
   c. Undefined
   d. Undefined

121. _____ is a subset of a population.
   a. Sample0
   b. Thing
   c. Undefined
   d. Undefined

122. _____ of a single or multiple future payments is the nominal amounts of money to change hands at some future date, discounted to account for the time value of money, and other factors such as investment risk.
   a. Present value0
   b. Thing
   c. Undefined
   d. Undefined

Chapter 9. The Trigonometric Functions

1. _____ is the process of planning, recording, and controlling the movement of a craft or vehicle from one place to another.
   a. Thing
   b. Navigation0
   c. Undefined
   d. Undefined

2. The _____ of measurement are a globally standardized and modernized form of the metric system.
   a. Units0
   b. Thing
   c. Undefined
   d. Undefined

3. The _____ is a unit of plane angle. It is represented by the symbol "rad" or, more rarely, by the superscript c (for "circular measure"). For example, an angle of 1.2 radians would be written "1.2 rad" or "1.2c" (second symbol can produce confusion with centigrads).
   a. Thing
   b. Radian0
   c. Undefined
   d. Undefined

4. _____ is a unit of plane angle, equal to 180/δ degrees, or about 57.2958 degrees
   a. Thing
   b. Radian measure0
   c. Undefined
   d. Undefined

5. A _____ was a citizen of Babylonia, named for its capital city, Babylon, which was an ancient state in the south part of Mesopotamia (in modern Iraq), combining the territories of Sumer and Akkad.
   a. Babylonian0
   b. Place
   c. Undefined
   d. Undefined

6. A _____ is a function that assigns a number to subsets of a given set.
   a. Measure0
   b. Thing
   c. Undefined
   d. Undefined

7. _____ is the estimation of a physical quantity such as distance, energy, temperature, or time.
   a. Thing
   b. Measurement0
   c. Undefined
   d. Undefined

8. In mathematics, there are several meanings of _____ depending on the subject.
   a. Thing
   b. Degree0
   c. Undefined
   d. Undefined

9. _____ are a measure of time.
   a. Minutes0
   b. Thing
   c. Undefined
   d. Undefined

10. In mathematics, the _____ functions are functions of an angle; they are important when studying triangles and modeling periodic phenomena, among many other applications.
    a. Thing
    b. Trigonometric0
    c. Undefined
    d. Undefined

11. The _____ are functions of an angle; they are important when studying triangles and modeling periodic phenomena, among many other applications.

Chapter 9. The Trigonometric Functions

   a. Thing
   c. Undefined
   b. Trigonometric functions0
   d. Undefined

12. _____ is a mathematical subject that includes the study of limits, derivatives, integrals, and power series and constitutes a major part of modern university curriculum.
   a. Thing
   c. Undefined
   b. Calculus0
   d. Undefined

13. _____, a field in mathematics, is the study of how functions change when their inputs change. The primary object of study in _____ is the derivative.
   a. Differential calculus0
   c. Undefined
   b. Thing
   d. Undefined

14. The mathematical concept of a _____ expresses the intuitive idea of deterministic dependence between two quantities, one of which is viewed as primary and the other as secondary. A _____ then is a way to associate a unique output for each input of a specified type, for example, a real number or an element of a given set.
   a. Thing
   c. Undefined
   b. Function0
   d. Undefined

15. In Euclidean geometry, an _____ is a closed segment of a differentiable curve in the two-dimensional plane; for example, a circular _____ is a segment of a circle.
   a. Concept
   c. Undefined
   b. Arc0
   d. Undefined

16. _____ is an adjective usually refering to being in the centre.
   a. Central0
   c. Undefined
   b. Thing
   d. Undefined

17. The _____ is the distance around a closed curve. _____ is a kind of perimeter.
   a. Circumference0
   c. Undefined
   b. Thing
   d. Undefined

18. In Euclidean geometry, a _____ is the set of all points in a plane at a fixed distance, called the radius, from a given point, the center.
   a. Circle0
   c. Undefined
   b. Thing
   d. Undefined

19. In classical geometry, a _____ of a circle or sphere is any line segment from its center to its boundary. By extension, the _____ of a circle or sphere is the length of any such segment. The _____ is half the diameter. In science and engineering the term _____ of curvature is commonly used as a synonym for _____.
   a. Thing
   c. Undefined
   b. Radius0
   d. Undefined

20. A _____ is one of the basic shapes of geometry: a polygon with three vertices and three sides which are straight line segments.

a. Triangle0
b. Thing
c. Undefined
d. Undefined

21. _____ has one 90° internal angle a right angle.
   a. Right triangle0
   b. Thing
   c. Undefined
   d. Undefined

22. A _____ is the result of the addition of a set of numbers. The numbers may be natural numbers, complex numbers, matrices, or still more complicated objects. An infinite _____ is a subtle procedure known as a series.
   a. Thing
   b. Sum0
   c. Undefined
   d. Undefined

23. In geometry and trigonometry, a _____ is defined as an angle between two straight intersecting lines of ninety degrees, or one-quarter of a circle.
   a. Thing
   b. Right angle0
   c. Undefined
   d. Undefined

24. A _____ is a movement of an object in a circular motion. A two-dimensional object rotates around a center (or point) of _____. A three-dimensional object rotates around a line called an axis. If the axis of _____ is within the body, the body is said to rotate upon itself, or spin—which implies relative speed and perhaps free-movement with angular momentum. A circular motion about an external point, e.g. the Earth about the Sun, is called an orbit or more properly an orbital revolution.
   a. Rotation0
   b. Thing
   c. Undefined
   d. Undefined

25. In geometry, a line _____ is a part of a line that is bounded by two end points, and contains every point on the line between its end points.
   a. Concept
   b. Segment0
   c. Undefined
   d. Undefined

26. _____ is a trigonemtric function that is important when studying triangles and modeling periodic phenomena, among other applications.
   a. Thing
   b. Sine0
   c. Undefined
   d. Undefined

27. A _____ is a set of numbers that designate location in a given reference system, such as x,y in a planar _____ system or an x,y,z in a three-dimensional _____ system.
   a. Thing
   b. Coordinate0
   c. Undefined
   d. Undefined

28. The _____ of an angle is the ratio of the length of the adjacent side to the length of the hypotenuse.
   a. Concept
   b. Cosine0
   c. Undefined
   d. Undefined

29. A _____ is a quantity that denotes the proportional amount or magnitude of one quantity relative to another.

Chapter 9. The Trigonometric Functions 105

   a. Ratio0
   c. Undefined
   b. Thing
   d. Undefined

30. A _____ is a simplified and structured visual representation of concepts, ideas, constructions, relations, statistical data, anatomy etc used in all aspects of human activities to visualize and clarify the topic.
   a. Thing
   c. Undefined
   b. Diagram0
   d. Undefined

31. A _____ given two distinct points A and B on the _____, is the set of points C on the line containing points A and B such that A is not strictly between C and B.
   a. Thing
   c. Undefined
   b. Ray0
   d. Undefined

32. A _____ is a deliberate process for transforming one or more inputs into one or more results.
   a. Thing
   c. Undefined
   b. Calculation0
   d. Undefined

33. In mathematics, the additive inverse, or _____ of a number n is the number that, when added to n, yields zero. The additive inverse of n is denoted −n. For example, 7 is −7, because 7 + (−7) = 0, and the additive inverse of −0.3 is 0.3, because −0.3 + 0.3 = 0.
   a. Opposite0
   c. Undefined
   b. Thing
   d. Undefined

34. The _____ of a right triangle is the triangle's longest side; the side opposite the right angle.
   a. Thing
   c. Undefined
   b. Hypotenuse0
   d. Undefined

35. In mathematics, the _____ of a number n is the number that, when added to n, yields zero. The _____ of n is denoted −n. For example, 7 is −7, because 7 + (−7) = 0, and the _____ of −0.3 is 0.3, because −0.3 + 0.3 = 0.
   a. Additive inverse0
   c. Undefined
   b. Thing
   d. Undefined

36. In geometry, _____ angles are angles that have a common ray coming out of the vertex going between two other rays.
   a. Adjacent0
   c. Undefined
   b. Concept
   d. Undefined

37. _____ is a circle with a unit radius, i.e., a circle whose radius is 1.
   a. Unit circle0
   c. Undefined
   b. Thing
   d. Undefined

38. In mathematics, a _____ (also spelled reflexion) is a map that transforms an object into its mirror image.
   a. Reflection0
   c. Undefined
   b. Concept
   d. Undefined

Chapter 9. The Trigonometric Functions

39. An _____ is an equality that remains true regardless of the values of any variables that appear within it, to distinguish it from an equality which is true under more particular conditions.
  a. Identity0
  b. Thing
  c. Undefined
  d. Undefined

40. _____ is a branch of mathematics which deals with triangles, particularly triangles in a plane where one angle of the triangle is 90 degrees, and a variety of other topological relations such as spheres, in other branches, such as spherical _____.
  a. Trigonometry0
  b. Thing
  c. Undefined
  d. Undefined

41. In mathematics, a _____ is a demonstration that, assuming certain axioms, some statement is necessarily true.
  a. Proof0
  b. Thing
  c. Undefined
  d. Undefined

42. In business, particularly accounting, a _____ is the time intervals that the accounts, statement, payments, or other calculations cover.
  a. Thing
  b. Period0
  c. Undefined
  d. Undefined

43. Mathematical _____ is used to represent ideas.
  a. Thing
  b. Notation0
  c. Undefined
  d. Undefined

44. A _____ is a symbolic representation denoting a quantity or expression. It often represents an "unknown" quantity that has the potential to change.
  a. Variable0
  b. Thing
  c. Undefined
  d. Undefined

45. In mathematics, an _____ is any of the arguments, i.e. "inputs", to a function. Thus if we have a function f(x), then x is a _____.
  a. Thing
  b. Independent variable0
  c. Undefined
  d. Undefined

46. _____ is a physical property of a system that underlies the common notions of hot and cold; something that is hotter has the greater _____.
  a. Temperature0
  b. Thing
  c. Undefined
  d. Undefined

47. _____ is a temperature scale named after the German physicist Daniel Gabriel _____, who proposed it in 1724.
  a. Fahrenheit0
  b. Thing
  c. Undefined
  d. Undefined

48. _____ is a state located in the southern and southwestern regions of the United States of America.

Chapter 9. The Trogonometric Functions

a. Texas0
b. Thing
c. Undefined
d. Undefined

49. In mathematics, the _____ of a function is the set of all "output" values produced by that function. Given a function $f : A \to B$, the _____ of f, is defined to be the set $\{x \in B : x = f(a) \text{ for some } a \in A\}$.
    a. Range0
    b. Thing
    c. Undefined
    d. Undefined

50. In linear algebra, the _____ of an n-by-n square matrix A is defined to be the sum of the elements on the main diagonal of A,
    a. Thing
    b. Trace0
    c. Undefined
    d. Undefined

51. In geographic information systems, a _____ comprises an entity with a geographic location, typically determined by points, arcs, or polygons. Carriageways and cadastres exemplify _____ data.
    a. Feature0
    b. Thing
    c. Undefined
    d. Undefined

52. _____ is a kind of property which exists as magnitude or multitude. It is among the basic classes of things along with quality, substance, change, and relation.
    a. Amount0
    b. Thing
    c. Undefined
    d. Undefined

53. A _____ is a part of a line that is bounded by two end points, and contains every point on the line between its end points.
    a. Thing
    b. Line segment0
    c. Undefined
    d. Undefined

54. _____ is often used to describe the measurement of the steepness, incline, gradient, or grade of a straight line. The _____ is defined as the ratio of the "rise" divided by the "run" between two points on a line, or in other words, the ratio of the altitude change to the horizontal distance between any two points on the line.
    a. Thing
    b. Slope0
    c. Undefined
    d. Undefined

55. In mathematics, the concept of a _____ tries to capture the intuitive idea of a geometrical one-dimensional and continuous object. A simple example is the circle.
    a. Curve0
    b. Thing
    c. Undefined
    d. Undefined

56. A _____ is a negotiable instrument instructing a financial institution to pay a specific amount of a specific currency from a specific demand account held in the maker/depositor's name with that institution. Both the maker and payee may be natural persons or legal entities.
    a. Check0
    b. Thing
    c. Undefined
    d. Undefined

57. The _____ is a measurement of how a function changes when the values of its inputs change.

a. Thing
b. Derivative0
c. Undefined
d. Undefined

58. _____ is a process of combining or accumulating. It may also refer to:
a. Thing
b. Integration0
c. Undefined
d. Undefined

59. The _____, the average in everyday English, which is also called the arithmetic _____ (and is distinguished from the geometric _____ or harmonic _____). The average is also called the sample _____. The expected value of a random variable, which is also called the population _____.
a. Mean0
b. Thing
c. Undefined
d. Undefined

60. In mathematics, a _____ is the result of multiplying, or an expression that identifies factors to be multiplied.
a. Product0
b. Thing
c. Undefined
d. Undefined

61. The _____ governs the differentiation of products of differentiable functions.
a. Thing
b. Product rule0
c. Undefined
d. Undefined

62. In mathematics, a _____ is the end result of a division problem. It can also be expressed as the number of times the divisor divides into the dividend.
a. Thing
b. Quotient0
c. Undefined
d. Undefined

63. The _____ is a method of finding the derivative of a function that is the quotient of two other functions for which derivatives exist.
a. Thing
b. Quotient rule0
c. Undefined
d. Undefined

64. _____ is the ability to hold, receive or absorb, or a measure thereof, similar to the concept of volume.
a. Concept
b. Capacity0
c. Undefined
d. Undefined

65. The _____ of a solid object is the three-dimensional concept of how much space it occupies, often quantified numerically.
a. Volume0
b. Thing
c. Undefined
d. Undefined

66. In mathematics and the mathematical sciences, a _____ is a fixed, but possibly unspecified, value. This is in contrast to a variable, which is not fixed.
a. Constant0
b. Thing
c. Undefined
d. Undefined

67. An _____ of a function f is a function F whose derivative is equal to f, i.e., F' = f.

Chapter 9. The Trigonometric Functions

a. Antiderivative0
b. Thing
c. Undefined
d. Undefined

68. A _____ is an abstract model that uses mathematical language to describe the behavior of a system. Eykhoff defined a _____ as 'a representation of the essential aspects of an existing system which presents knowledge of that system in usable form'.
   a. Thing
   b. Mathematical model0
   c. Undefined
   d. Undefined

69. A _____ is a function that repeats its values after some definite period has been added to its independent variable.
   a. Periodic function0
   b. Thing
   c. Undefined
   d. Undefined

70. A _____ is a special kind of ratio, indicating a relationship between two measurements with different units, such as miles to gallons or cents to pounds.
   a. Thing
   b. Rate0
   c. Undefined
   d. Undefined

71. In elementary algebra, an _____ is a set that contains every real number between two indicated numbers and may contain the two numbers themselves.
   a. Thing
   b. Interval0
   c. Undefined
   d. Undefined

72. In mathematics, an _____, mean, or central tendency of a data set refers to a measure of the "middle" or "expected" value of the data set.
   a. Average0
   b. Concept
   c. Undefined
   d. Undefined

73. In sociology and biology a _____ is the collection of people or organisms of a particular species living in a given geographic area or space, usually measured by a census.
   a. Population0
   b. Thing
   c. Undefined
   d. Undefined

74. In trigonometry, the _____ is a function defined as $\tan x = \sin x / \cos x$. The function is so-named because it can be defined as the length of a certain segment of a _____ (in the geometric sense) to the unit circle. In plane geometry, a line is _____ to a curve, at some point, if both line and curve pass through the point with the same direction.
   a. Tangent0
   b. Thing
   c. Undefined
   d. Undefined

75. _____ has two distinct but etymologically-related meanings: one in geometry and one in trigonometry.
   a. Thing
   b. Tangent line0
   c. Undefined
   d. Undefined

76. _____ is a trigonometric function that is the reciprocal of cosine.

a. Secant0
b. Thing
c. Undefined
d. Undefined

77. _____ of a curve is a line that intersects two or more points on the curve.
   a. Secant line0
   b. Thing
   c. Undefined
   d. Undefined

78. In mathematics, science including computer science, linguistics and engineering, an _____ is, generally speaking, an independent variable or input to a function.
   a. Thing
   b. Argument0
   c. Undefined
   d. Undefined

79. The _____ of a function is an extension of the concept of a sum, and are identified or found through the use of integration.
   a. Integral0
   b. Thing
   c. Undefined
   d. Undefined

80. In mathematics, factorization (British English: factorisation) or factoring is the decomposition of an object (for example, a number, a polynomial, or a matrix) into a product of other objects, or _____, which when multiplied together give the original.
   a. Thing
   b. Factors0
   c. Undefined
   d. Undefined

81. In calculus, the _____ is a formula for the derivative of the composite of two functions.
   a. Chain rule0
   b. Concept
   c. Undefined
   d. Undefined

82. _____ is a term in Trigonometry used to describe the secant of the complement of a cirlce.
   a. Thing
   b. Cosecant0
   c. Undefined
   d. Undefined

83. _____ is the ratio of the adjacent to the opposite side of a right-angeled triangle
   a. Cotangent0
   b. Thing
   c. Undefined
   d. Undefined

84. A _____ is the part of a fraction that tells how many equal parts make up a whole, and which is used in the name of the fraction: "halves", "thirds", "fourths" or "quarters", "fifths" and so on.
   a. Denominator0
   b. Concept
   c. Undefined
   d. Undefined

85. The _____ of a geographic location is its height above a fixed reference point, often the mean sea level.
   a. Elevation0
   b. Thing
   c. Undefined
   d. Undefined

86. Equivalence is the condition of being _____ or essentially equal.

Chapter 9. The Trigonometric Functions

a. Thing
c. Undefined
b. Equivalent0
d. Undefined

87. _____ has many meanings, most of which simply .
a. Thing
c. Undefined
b. Power0
d. Undefined

88. _____ is a method for differentiating expressions involving exponentiation the power operation.
a. Power rule0
c. Undefined
b. Thing
d. Undefined

89. A pair of angles is _____ if their respective measures sum to 180 degrees.
a. Concept
c. Undefined
b. Supplementary0
d. Undefined

90. _____ are the basic objects of study in graph theory. Informally speaking, a graph is a set of objects called points, nodes, or vertices connected by links called lines or edges.
a. Thing
c. Undefined
b. Graphs0
d. Undefined

91. In astronomy, geography, geometry and related sciences and contexts, a plane is said to be _____ at a given point if it is locally perpendicular to the gradient of the gravity field, i.e., with the direction of the gravitational force at that point.
a. Thing
c. Undefined
b. Horizontal0
d. Undefined

92. A _____ is traditionally an infinitesimally small change in a variable.
a. Differential0
c. Undefined
b. Thing
d. Undefined

93. A _____ is a mathematical equation for an unknown function of one or several variables which relates the values of the function itself and of its derivatives of various orders.
a. Thing
c. Undefined
b. Differential equation0
d. Undefined

94. _____ is a a point on a curve at which the tangent crosses the curve itself.
a. Inflection point0
c. Undefined
b. Thing
d. Undefined

95. In mathematics, _____ are the intuitive idea of a geometrical one-dimensional and continuous object.
a. Curves0
c. Undefined
b. Thing
d. Undefined

96. In mathematical analysis and related areas of mathematics, a set is called _____, if it is, in a certain sense, of finite size.

a. Thing
b. Bounded0
c. Undefined
d. Undefined

ANSWER KEY

Chapter 1

1. a	2. a	3. b	4. a	5. b	6. a	7. a	8. b	9. a	10. b
11. b	12. b	13. a	14. b	15. b	16. a	17. a	18. a	19. b	20. a
21. b	22. a	23. b	24. b	25. b	26. b	27. a	28. b	29. b	30. b
31. b	32. b	33. a	34. a	35. b	36. a	37. a	38. b	39. a	40. b
41. a	42. b	43. b	44. b	45. a	46. b	47. a	48. b	49. a	50. b
51. b	52. a	53. a	54. a	55. a	56. a	57. b	58. a	59. a	60. b
61. b	62. b	63. a	64. b	65. a	66. a	67. b	68. b	69. a	70. b
71. a	72. a	73. b	74. b	75. b	76. b	77. a	78. b	79. b	80. b
81. b	82. a	83. b	84. b	85. b	86. b	87. b	88. b	89. a	90. b
91. a	92. b	93. b	94. b	95. b	96. b	97. b	98. b	99. a	100. a
101. a	102. a	103. b	104. a	105. b	106. a	107. a	108. b	109. b	110. a
111. b	112. a	113. a	114. a	115. b	116. a	117. b	118. b	119. a	120. a
121. b	122. b	123. a	124. a	125. b	126. b	127. b	128. a	129. a	130. b
131. b	132. b	133. a	134. a	135. b	136. a	137. b	138. b	139. a	140. b
141. a	142. a	143. b	144. b	145. a	146. a	147. b	148. b	149. b	150. a

Chapter 2

1. b	2. b	3. b	4. b	5. a	6. a	7. a	8. b	9. a	10. b
11. b	12. a	13. a	14. b	15. b	16. a	17. b	18. b	19. a	20. a
21. a	22. a	23. b	24. b	25. b	26. b	27. a	28. b	29. a	30. a
31. b	32. a	33. a	34. a	35. a	36. a	37. a	38. a	39. a	40. b
41. a	42. a	43. a	44. b	45. b	46. b	47. a	48. a	49. b	50. a
51. b	52. a	53. a	54. a	55. b	56. b	57. b	58. b	59. b	60. b
61. b	62. b	63. b	64. a	65. b	66. a	67. b	68. a	69. b	70. b
71. a	72. a	73. a	74. a	75. b	76. a	77. a	78. b	79. b	80. a
81. b	82. a	83. b	84. b	85. b	86. b	87. a	88. a	89. b	90. b
91. b	92. b	93. b	94. a	95. a	96. a	97. b	98. b	99. b	100. a
101. b	102. a								

Chapter 3

1. a	2. a	3. a	4. a	5. b	6. b	7. b	8. a	9. a	10. b
11. a	12. b	13. b	14. b	15. b	16. b	17. b	18. a	19. a	20. b
21. b	22. a	23. b	24. a	25. a	26. a	27. a	28. a	29. b	30. a
31. b	32. b	33. b	34. a	35. b	36. a	37. b	38. b	39. a	40. a
41. a	42. a	43. b	44. a	45. a	46. a	47. a	48. a	49. b	50. b
51. a	52. a	53. a	54. b	55. a	56. b	57. b	58. b	59. b	60. a
61. a	62. a	63. a	64. a	65. a	66. a	67. a	68. a	69. a	70. b
71. a	72. a	73. b	74. b	75. b	76. b	77. b	78. b	79. b	80. a
81. a	82. a	83. a	84. b	85. b	86. b	87. b	88. b	89. a	90. b
91. b	92. b	93. b	94. a	95. b	96. a	97. b	98. b	99. b	100. b
101. b	102. a	103. a	104. b	105. b	106. a	107. b	108. a	109. b	110. b
111. b	112. b	113. a	114. a	115. a	116. a	117. b	118. b	119. b	120. a
121. a	122. a	123. b	124. b	125. a	126. a				

Chapter 4

1. b	2. b	3. a	4. a	5. b	6. b	7. a	8. b	9. a	10. b
11. a	12. b	13. b	14. a	15. b	16. b	17. a	18. a	19. b	20. a
21. b	22. b	23. a	24. a	25. a	26. a	27. a	28. a	29. b	30. a
31. b	32. a	33. b	34. a	35. a	36. b	37. a	38. b	39. a	40. a
41. b	42. a	43. a	44. b	45. b	46. a	47. b	48. a	49. a	50. a
51. a	52. b	53. b	54. b	55. a	56. a	57. b	58. a	59. b	60. b
61. a	62. b	63. b	64. b	65. b	66. a	67. b	68. b	69. a	70. b
71. a	72. b	73. a	74. b	75. a	76. b	77. b	78. b	79. b	80. a
81. b	82. a	83. b	84. a	85. b	86. b	87. a	88. a	89. a	90. b
91. a									

Chapter 5

1. b	2. b	3. b	4. b	5. a	6. a	7. a	8. b	9. b	10. b
11. a	12. a	13. a	14. a	15. a	16. b	17. b	18. b	19. b	20. b
21. b	22. a	23. a	24. a	25. a	26. b	27. a	28. b	29. b	30. b
31. a	32. b	33. b	34. a	35. a	36. b	37. a	38. b	39. b	40. b
41. b	42. b	43. a	44. a	45. a	46. a	47. b	48. a	49. a	50. a
51. a	52. b	53. a	54. b	55. a	56. b	57. a	58. a	59. a	60. b
61. a	62. b	63. b	64. b	65. a	66. a	67. a	68. b	69. a	70. b
71. b	72. b	73. b	74. a	75. a	76. a	77. a	78. a	79. b	80. a
81. b	82. a	83. b	84. b	85. b	86. b	87. a			

Chapter 6

1. a	2. a	3. a	4. a	5. a	6. a	7. a	8. b	9. b	10. a
11. b	12. b	13. b	14. a	15. a	16. b	17. b	18. a	19. b	20. b
21. b	22. b	23. a	24. b	25. a	26. a	27. a	28. b	29. b	30. b
31. a	32. a	33. b	34. b	35. a	36. b	37. a	38. b	39. b	40. a
41. b	42. a	43. a	44. b	45. a	46. a	47. b	48. a	49. b	50. b
51. b	52. a	53. b	54. b	55. b	56. a	57. a	58. a	59. b	60. a
61. a	62. a	63. a	64. b	65. b	66. b	67. a	68. b	69. b	70. b
71. a	72. b	73. b	74. a	75. a	76. b	77. a	78. b	79. a	80. b
81. a	82. a	83. b	84. a	85. b	86. b	87. b	88. a	89. b	90. a
91. a	92. b	93. b	94. a	95. a	96. b	97. a	98. b		

ANSWER KEY

Chapter 7

1. a	2. b	3. a	4. b	5. a	6. b	7. b	8. b	9. a	10. a
11. b	12. a	13. a	14. b	15. a	16. b	17. b	18. a	19. a	20. a
21. a	22. b	23. a	24. b	25. a	26. a	27. b	28. a	29. a	30. a
31. a	32. b	33. a	34. b	35. a	36. b	37. a	38. a	39. a	40. b
41. b	42. b	43. a	44. b	45. b	46. b	47. b	48. b	49. a	50. b
51. a	52. a	53. a	54. b	55. a	56. a	57. b	58. a	59. b	60. b
61. b	62. a	63. a	64. a	65. b	66. a	67. b	68. a	69. b	70. a
71. a	72. a	73. b	74. a	75. a	76. b	77. b	78. b	79. a	80. a
81. b	82. a	83. a	84. a	85. b	86. b	87. b	88. a	89. b	90. b
91. a	92. b	93. b	94. a	95. b	96. b	97. a	98. b	99. a	100. a
101. b	102. a	103. a	104. b	105. a	106. b	107. a	108. a	109. b	110. a
111. a	112. b	113. a	114. b	115. b	116. b	117. b	118. a	119. b	120. b
121. b	122. a	123. b	124. b	125. b	126. a	127. a	128. b	129. a	130. b
131. a	132. a	133. b	134. b	135. b	136. b	137. b	138. a	139. a	140. a
141. b	142. a	143. a	144. b	145. b	146. b	147. b	148. b	149. b	

Chapter 8

1. a	2. b	3. b	4. b	5. a	6. a	7. b	8. a	9. a	10. a
11. b	12. b	13. a	14. a	15. b	16. b	17. a	18. b	19. a	20. b
21. a	22. a	23. b	24. a	25. a	26. a	27. b	28. b	29. a	30. b
31. b	32. a	33. b	34. b	35. a	36. b	37. a	38. b	39. a	40. a
41. b	42. b	43. b	44. a	45. b	46. b	47. a	48. a	49. a	50. b
51. a	52. b	53. b	54. a	55. a	56. b	57. a	58. a	59. b	60. b
61. a	62. b	63. a	64. a	65. b	66. b	67. b	68. b	69. a	70. a
71. b	72. a	73. a	74. a	75. b	76. a	77. b	78. a	79. b	80. b
81. b	82. a	83. a	84. a	85. a	86. a	87. b	88. a	89. b	90. a
91. b	92. b	93. a	94. a	95. b	96. a	97. b	98. b	99. a	100. b
101. b	102. b	103. b	104. b	105. a	106. a	107. b	108. b	109. a	110. a
111. b	112. a	113. a	114. b	115. b	116. a	117. a	118. a	119. b	120. b
121. a	122. a								

Chapter 9

1. b	2. a	3. b	4. b	5. a	6. a	7. b	8. b	9. a	10. b
11. b	12. b	13. a	14. b	15. b	16. a	17. a	18. a	19. b	20. a
21. a	22. b	23. b	24. a	25. b	26. b	27. b	28. b	29. a	30. b
31. b	32. b	33. a	34. b	35. a	36. a	37. a	38. a	39. a	40. a
41. a	42. b	43. b	44. a	45. b	46. a	47. a	48. a	49. a	50. b
51. a	52. a	53. b	54. b	55. a	56. a	57. b	58. b	59. a	60. a
61. b	62. b	63. b	64. b	65. a	66. a	67. a	68. b	69. a	70. b
71. b	72. a	73. a	74. a	75. b	76. a	77. a	78. b	79. a	80. b
81. a	82. b	83. a	84. a	85. a	86. b	87. b	88. a	89. b	90. b
91. b	92. a	93. b	94. a	95. a	96. b				

www.ingramcontent.com/pod-product-compliance
Lightning Source LLC
Chambersburg PA
CBHW082050230426
43670CB00016B/2838